JUST EMOTIONS

CLARENDON STUDIES IN CRIMINOLOGY

Published under the auspices of the Institute of Criminology, University of Cambridge; the Mannheim Centre, London School of Economics; and the Centre for Criminological Research, University of Oxford.

General Editor: Robert Reiner
(London School of Economics)

Editors: Manuel Eisner, Alison Liebling, and Per-Olof Wikström
(University of Cambridge)

Jill Peay and Tim Newburn
(London School of Economics)

Ian Loader, Julian Roberts, and Lucia Zedner
(University of Oxford)

RECENT TITLES IN THIS SERIES:

Just Emotions

Rituals of Restorative Justice

MEREDITH ROSSNER

OXFORD
UNIVERSITY PRESS

Great Clarendon Street, Oxford, OX2 6DP,
United Kingdom

Oxford University Press is a department of the University of Oxford.
It furthers the University's objective of excellence in research, scholarship,
and education by publishing worldwide. Oxford is a registered trade mark of
Oxford University Press in the UK and in certain other countries

© Meredith Rossner 2013

The moral rights of the author have been asserted

First Edition published in 2013

Impression: 1

Published in the United States of America by Oxford University Press
198 Madison Avenue, New York, NY 10016, United States of America

British Library Cataloguing in Publication Data
Data available

Library of Congress Control Number: 2013939664

ISBN 978–0–19–965504–5

Printed and bound in Great Britain by
CPI Group (UK) Ltd, Croydon, CR0 4YY

General Editor's Introduction

Clarendon Studies in Criminology aims to provide a forum for outstanding empirical and theoretical work in all aspects of criminology and criminal justice, broadly understood. The Editors welcome submissions from established scholars, as well as excellent PhD work. The *Series* was inaugurated in 1994, with Roger Hood as its first General Editor, following discussions between Oxford University Press and three criminology centres. It is edited under the auspices of these three centres: the Cambridge Institute of Criminology, the Mannheim Centre for Criminology at the London School of Economics, and the Centre for Criminology at the University of Oxford. Each supplies members of the Editorial Board and, in turn, the Series Editor.

Recent decades have seen penal policy and criminal justice increasingly dominated by rhetoric and practices assuming a zero-sum conflict between offenders and victims, with concern for the latter only capable of being served by getting tough on the former. In this harsh climate restorative justice has been the main hope of those who wish to preserve more humane and optimistic possibilities. It has become increasingly influential amongst policy-makers and practitioners around the world, promising not only more humane alternatives to punitiveness, but greater effectiveness achieved at less expense (this being a primary concern to governments obsessed by austerity).

Meredith Rossner's *Just Emotions: Rituals of Restorative Justice* is an important and innovative contribution to the burgeoning literature on restorative justice. It is a highly sensitive, nuanced, and perceptive micro sociology of the emotional and interactive elements of restorative justice conferences. The book's central focus is on what enables some restorative justice conferences to become transformative events for offenders and victims, with the potential to reduce offending. Dr Rossner argues that the emotional and ritual dynamics within the restorative justice conference hold the key to success. She analyses how a dynamic process of building rhythm and a shared focus over time in the conference can generate solidarity between victims, offenders, their supporters, and the facilitators, as well as reintegration of offenders with their supporting networks following the stigmatization of conviction. It is this solidarity that can promote long-term emotional well-being as well as the holy grail of reduced offending in the future.

The analysis is based on a variety of sources, close observation of conferences and of video recordings, qualitative interviews with participants, and the RISE study—a larger-scale body of data from Australia. The book combines qualitative and quantitative methodologies. The hypotheses about emotional dynamics that succeed (or fail) to produce beneficial emotional and behavioural consequences that are teased out from exceptionally sensitive interpretation of observed interactions are tested by statistical analysis of the elements of the larger sample of conferences reported in the RISE study.

Dr Rossner's book demonstrates considerable scholarly and intellectual talents in probing deeply important but elusive encounters and issues. It is written with clarity and verve, and makes compelling reading (the author's academic background is in literature as well as criminology). It will be an important source not only for criminologists, but for policy-makers and practitioners, with user-friendly conclusions about how best to develop successful conferences. The Editors welcome it as a significant addition to the *Clarendon Studies in Criminology Series*.

Robert Reiner
London School of Economics
May 2013

Foreword

The potential for restorative justice to change the lives of victims and offenders has long been recognized. The prospect of it changing the lives of those engaged in research about it may seem less plausible. However, those of us who came together in London in the early years of this century to conduct the research that Meredith Rossner reports on here were all changed in some way by the experience. Our team, of which Meredith was a crucial member, was bound together by a commitment to achieving the very best quality scientific research. We were also bound by our sense that we were creating events that were hugely important to the people who agreed to participate in our experiments. Meredith brought to the project great energy and a fresh view. Her focus on the tiny details of each restorative justice encounter was one that had been largely neglected, though the important contribution of Tom Scheff and Suzanne Retzinger in the late 1990s is rightly acknowledged in this book. It was Meredith who grasped the importance of a micro sociological perspective on what happened in restorative justice ('RJ') meetings. From what she observed of the rituals of RJ—conversation, gesture, facial expression, demeanour, and dramatic interaction—and building on the work of Goffman and Collins, she has developed an original and important micro level theory of restorative justice. Meredith employs a mixed-methods approach, drawing on many sources including an analysis of the dynamics of a single conference that one of us observed in person. On that cold December night, the *dramatis personae* who nervously entered the meeting room did not appear a promising bunch; there was certainly no reason to expect that this would be an emotionally compelling event. Indeed it was not very different either in prospect or in execution from hundreds of other similar RJ meetings conducted in the course of our research. The only difference was that this one was filmed, giving Meredith the opportunity to extract miraculously revealing information from the event. 'Successful' or not in terms of reoffending—and at least in the two years after the conference no more offending was recorded—there was no doubt about the success of this meeting as a human drama. But that is not the point of this book and, as Meredith helps the reader to understand, good theatre does not automatically lead to life-changing behaviour. Thus, part of this book directly addresses this important subject: what are the short-term and long-term outcomes of 'good' and 'bad' RJ conferences? Drawing on our earlier experiments in Canberra, Meredith builds a convincing case that good conferences can create a strong sense of solidarity among all the parties present. She then shows that those meetings with high solidarity measures are followed by significantly less reoffending, at least over the following five years, than those with low solidarity.

This book is a remarkable and important contribution to the restorative justice literature, painstaking in its approach, measured in its conclusions. We are so glad to have worked with Meredith and warmly congratulate her on this outstanding contribution to the literature of micro sociology.

Heather Strang and Lawrence W Sherman
Institute of Criminology
Cambridge University
March 2013

Acknowledgements

This book has been made possible with the help and support of countless colleagues, mentors, and friends. I am indebted to the following for advice and comments at various stages of the research and writing process: Randall Collins, Lawrence Sherman, Heather Strang, Paul Rock, David Tait, Kathryn Edin, Jason Schnittker, John Braithwaite, Susanne Karstedt, David Gibson, Shadd Maruna, Frank Furstenberg, Sarah Bennett, Nova Inkpen, Janel Benson, Kristin Turney, Jacob Avery, Keith Brown, Evelyn Patterson, Jamie Fader, Dan Woods, Emily Turner, Carla Cue-Lewandowski, Arathi Sriprakash, Jasmine Bruce, Mythily Meher, and Madeline Kapira. In particular, Annee Lawrence deserves special thanks for her fantastic help with the editing and structuring of the manuscript. I have also benefitted enormously from the administrative support of Judy Camac, Carolanne Saunders, Janel McCaffrey-Baselice, and Knakiya Hagans.

Of course, much of the research would not be possible without the help of the Metropolitan Police in London. The police facilitators taught me how restorative justice can 'work' and I owe much to them. In particular, many of the ideas in this book arose from discussion over the years with Inspector Brian Dowling. Brian allowed me access to facilitators, restorative justice participants, and police files. He also provided valuable comments on earlier drafts.

I also thank colloquium participants at the Culture and Interaction Workshop at the University of Pennsylvania; Sydney University Law School, The Forum Sentencing Program at the New South Wales Department of Attorney General and Justice, Cambridge University, and the International Institute for the Sociology of Law at Onati, Spain.

Finally, I am grateful for the support of Ben Bramble and Joan, Steve, and Gertrude Rossner.

Contents

List of Figures and Tables

Figures

Tables

1

Introduction

A Transformative Event

Andrew[1] owed some money to Vincent and Charles, who were becoming increasingly angry at his failure to pay. One day the two of them concocted a plan to intimidate Andrew into paying up. All three boys were 18 years old, lived on the same London housing estate and knew of each other's comings and goings. Vince and Charles waited until Andrew came home and then broke into his flat and assaulted him. They tied him with cable and began beating him with the flat of a machete, all the while detailing how much harm he'd come to if he didn't pay. Afraid for his life, Andrew struggled to free himself and in a bid to escape fell to his death from his sixth floor balcony. While Vince and Charles maintained they never intended to kill Andrew, they were prosecuted for murder, eventually pleading guilty to manslaughter.

The effects of this tragic event rippled through the community. Andrew's mother, Doris, was inconsolable and in the months after her son's death she remained traumatized. She had emigrated from Nigeria with her children and had few friends in London. She'd known Andrew was hanging around with a rough crowd and even suspected he was involved in drugs or other illegal activities. However, although she knew how dangerous the neighbourhood had become, she didn't have the money to move elsewhere. Now Doris told herself that she should never have come to the UK, that if she and the children had stayed in Nigeria, Andrew would still be alive. During this difficult time the only thing giving Doris strength was her deep Christian faith but, despite this, her local chaplain and his wife were very worried that, because she blamed herself for what had happened to Andrew, she was showing no signs of recovery.

When the chaplain's wife heard about a Metropolitan Police experiment in restorative justice, where victims of crime and their

---

[1] Names throughout this book have been changed

families could meet face to face with their offenders, she approached the police. They agreed to organize a meeting between Doris and the two offenders, Vince and Charles, who were also the children of West African immigrants. By now the two men were serving six year sentences at a prison located four hours from London. They initially refused to take part in the restorative justice experiment but changed their minds after talking with inmates who had participated in similar conferences. With their agreement the police facilitator, Ben, invited Vince's mother and Charles's mother, aunt, uncle, and two sisters to come to the conference as well. The two families, one Christian and one Muslim, were both very religious. Although apprehensive and strongly distrustful of police, they agreed to participate after consulting their local imam and pastor. On the victim's side there was Doris, her remaining son Robert (Andrew's brother) and the pastor's wife. As Ben made travel arrangements for the various parties to get to the prison, he took care to stagger their arrival in order to avoid any awkward confrontations at the train station. On arrival at the prison, a guard ushered everyone into a small classroom in which some chairs had been arranged in a circle. Once they were all seated, Charles and Vince were brought into the room and quickly sat down with their families.

This was the cue for Ben to introduce everyone and begin the conference. Charles and Vince kept their heads down and were slightly slouched—too nervous and afraid to look anyone in the eye, including their own family members. Prompted by Ben, they explained what had happened. Although most people had heard the story in court, they were still moved to tears, with Doris crying the hardest as her surviving son tried to console her. Ben then asked Vince and Charles how they thought others were affected by what they had done. They immediately started apologizing to Doris, asking her to let them take all the responsibility and telling her that none of this was her fault or Andrew's fault.

Charles said, 'I just don't know how it would feel to lose a son who you have cared for. I guess it would upset my mum.' When he said this his mother began to cry. Then Doris asked, 'What on earth did he do to you to make you do this to him?' Charles replied, 'He didn't do anything to deserve this. This was us getting carried away.' Vince added,

I know that you would like a reason. But when I think about it, and I thought about it a lot in my cell, I can't think of one. We were just completely off our heads. We were stupid. We wanted to frighten him. But we didn't think one minute what he might do. We thought, let him think we are going to kill him. We never thought what he would do if he really believed it.

Vince's mother began to cry. Suddenly, Charles's mother rose up out of her seat, stepped forward and knelt down in front of Doris and began hugging her. Doris responded by hugging her back. By this time everybody was wiping the tears from their eyes. Ben then asked Robert to speak. At first he was reluctant to share his emotions, only speaking about his mother's pain. Eventually he began to reveal his sorrow and loneliness, explaining that he and Andrew used to share a bedroom. As they listened, Charles's two sisters cried and embraced each other.

With everybody quiet and respectfully listening, Charles's mother described the shame caused to her family by her son's actions. She acknowledged that while having a son in prison was hard, it was not the same as a son killed. Charles's uncle spoke next about the devastation to the family and provided a little background about Charles. He made a point not to do this in a defensive way, but just to 'paint a picture'. Charles's older sister dried her eyes and calmly spoke of how she 'spent a lot of time trying to be hard and tough' but was suffering on the inside.

Ben then turned to Charles's 14-year-old sister, Clarice. At first her mother had refused permission for her to participate, but Ben urged her to relent, suspecting that she would have a lot to contribute. He asked Clarice, 'How did you hear about this?' and she said, 'This is the first time I've heard any of this. Everybody is treating me like I'm a child, [but] he's my brother.' She went on to describe the police showing up at their house to take Charles away and her sadness and anger that she didn't have a chance to say goodbye. She complained that everybody was treating her like a child, not keeping her informed and not letting her share in the family pain, lamenting that she wasn't even allowed into the courtroom for her brother's trial or sentencing.

At this point, tears began to flow again and Clarice's aunt stood up to embrace her. Doris also stood, crossed the circle, and clasped the young woman's hand. According to Ben,

That was a defining moment. I think if you can get someone very emotional in a room, who talks very personally about what it meant to them, that becomes a defining moment. This was already very emotional, there was already a shared understanding. But this pushed it over the edge quite truly. This was now a group of people [who]...desperately wanted to move on from it and find something positive.

Moving into the final stage of the conference, the group began to discuss what Vince and Charles could do to repair the harm. After a productive discussion about what they could do in prison they agreed to talk to other inmates about restorative justice conferences in a prison workshop. This finished the formal part of the conference and it was announced the group would break for a cup of tea. At this point everybody spontaneously got up and started hugging and, as Ben observed, Vince and Charles and Doris even got 'close and exchanged knowing glances a few times. There was strong eye contact between them. It was probably a much more profound apology than anything they could have said.' There was a great deal of touching and shoulder rubbing. At the end, Andrew's brother shook hands with Vince and Charles.

Prior to the conference, Vince's mother had expressed her anxiety to Ben that Andrew's family would abuse her son and cause more traumas to the family. Now that it was over she and the others were smiling and happily talking. As Ben explained,

There was a lot of relief. Smiling. People telling each other how impressed they were that they were there and spoke. Particularly the little girl. She stopped the show. Everybody was nice to everybody.

To Ben's utter surprise, they decided to mark the end of the conference by praying together so the pastor's wife led them in a short prayer. Later, at the station, everyone went and sat in the same carriage for the train back to London.

Six months later, with tears in his eyes as he relived the conference, Ben described it to me as one of the best things he had done in more than twenty years as a police officer.

A Waste of Time

Tom was a middle class businessman who lived in a seaside town with his family. He worked in London during the week and spent his weekends at home. One evening after work he crossed the city to an area that is well known for its seedy nightlife. At around eleven pm, while coming out of a cinema, he was accosted by a young man who may have offered him sex for money (the details are unknown and this is speculation by the facilitator). Tom refused and began walking to the train station. A few moments later the young man reappeared, flashed a knife, and stole Tom's wallet. Tom, seeing a patrolling policeman, reluctantly reported the robbery and gave a description of his assailant. A few weeks later a police officer called to say that a man matching the description he'd given had been arrested and pleaded guilty to the robbery.

The young man's name was Sadiq and he was an Iraqi refugee. A police facilitator, Adam, informed Tom about a new restorative justice programme and offered him the opportunity to meet Sadiq face to face in a conference. After a long discussion in which Adam outlined the potential benefits to both the victim and the offender of participating, Tom agreed. Adam guessed, however, that Tom was embarrassed about what had happened and only agreed to the conference so he could be seen to be cooperating with the police. Tom had not told his wife, or anyone else, about the incident or the conference and he declined to ask any supporters along.

Adam then approached Sadiq who spoke little to no English. Adam thought that Sadiq was born in Iraq, but this could not be confirmed. It seemed that Sadiq's parents had sent him away when he was a small child and much of his youth had been spent in refugee camps throughout Europe. He had been in the UK for a few years but had no family and no identification. Without any passport or identifying information, Sadiq could not prove his refugee status, which meant he was precluded from working legally and unable to apply for any kind of public assistance. He was a man with no country, relatives, friends, or future and Adam thought he probably agreed to the restorative justice conference without any real understanding of what was being asked of him. He told Adam he was hoping for a custodial sentence so he would have somewhere to live.

The conference was held in the London prison where Sadiq was awaiting sentence for the offence. As well as arranging for an interpreter, Adam searched high and low for a supporter for Sadiq and, eventually, a volunteer at a homeless shelter where Sadiq once lived agreed to attend. All the participants arrived on time and the conference began promptly with Adam asking the usual initial questions to get the conversation going. His toolkit included various methods to encourage people to speak to each other, but none of these seemed to work in this conference. It was difficult to get the interaction to run smoothly and he tried to fill the silences by asking each of the two men a series of questions about the crime itself and how they were affected by it.

Both men responded with brief nods and one word answers, with no one uttering more than a sentence. Tom was reluctant to talk about any effects the robbery had on him, insisting that it was not a big deal and was just part of life in London. Sadiq, speaking through his interpreter, apologized for what he had done. He seemed to be sincerely sorry and Tom accepted his apology. They avoided eye contact and never exchanged more than a few words with each other. When they did speak they both focused their attention on Adam. Sadiq's supporter had next to nothing to contribute, adding that he barely knew Sadiq because he did not stand out in any way and was just one of many homeless men who seek refuge at the shelter.

After forty-five minutes of strained silences, the conference ended with the formal documentation that Sadiq had apologized and Tom had accepted his apology. Adam encouraged Sadiq and Tom to shake hands but they did this without looking at each other. Sadiq was led back to his cell and Tom went home as soon as possible.

Later, as we talked about it, Adam told me he had been embarrassed to facilitate such a conference because it felt so inappropriate. He felt it had all just been a 'waste of time'.

Spotting the Difference

The conferences described above, which resulted in dramatically different dynamics and outcomes, are reconstructed from in-depth interviews with the police who facilitated them and a review of case files from a restorative justice research programme in collaboration with the Metropolitan Police in London. In the first one, a direct connection was made between the victim and her family and the offenders and their families. There was a sense of profound symbolic reparation and a bringing together of people torn apart by tragedy. This was demonstrated by the apologies and expressions of remorse offered by the offenders, the spontaneous hugging, the group prayer, and the image of the families choosing to ride home in the same train carriage together.

The second encounter shared some of the traits of the first one. It seems possible that in both cases the victims were feeling a sense of shame—Doris was blaming herself for her son's death because she brought him to London and Tom was ashamed at the circumstances of his victimization, as demonstrated by his refusal to include his family in the process. The two conferences were held in a prison and were run by experienced police facilitators who met with everyone in advance, explained what would happen, and did their best to prepare the participants. They both started out uncomfortable, with inarticulate offenders not knowing what to say, but the first one 'took off' while the second suffered from excruciating long and embarrassed silences, no breakthrough of shared understanding, and no sense of symbolic reparation or togetherness.

What were the key elements that led to such dramatically different outcomes? Was it because of the individual characteristics of the participants involved? Were Vince and Charles somehow 'better' offenders? Was Sadiq not remorseful enough? Were they able to communicate properly? Did it have something to do with the characteristics of the offence? What role did the presence, or absence, of families play?

These, and other questions, will be explored in this book. While these outcomes may appear random, or the product of individual characteristics or personality differences, according to the theories presented in this book the sequence and flow of these interactions are patterned, ritualized, and relatively predictable. In other words, one can isolate the components of a 'good' interaction, for example, the development of conversational and bodily rhythm, a balance of power and perspective among participants, and a shared focus of their emotions.

Meetings like this are currently happening all over the world for different types of offences—for juveniles and adults, in prisons and in communities, at many different stages of the justice process. This process, called restorative justice, has the potential to offer a new kind of justice to victims, offenders, and communities.

Restorative justice has emerged as a hugely popular new paradigm of justice in recent decades. It may be the only criminal justice initiative that is truly bi-partisan—conservatives see it as an approach that makes offenders accountable and gives victims a voice, while liberals agree that it does all these things while, at the same time, empowering offenders and communities. However, when it is put into practice a wide variety of different processes and outcomes can be seen, both at the macro level in terms of the operational and organizational procedures, and at the micro level in terms of how the interactions, emotions, and dynamics play out.

This book examines what happens at the micro level. I suggest that background variables, such as the details of the crime or the demographic characteristics of the participants, are not the primary influences in determining success in restorative justice. Instead,

I move to the foreground of the meeting itself and its situational dynamics to explain how restorative justice works.

What is Restorative Justice?

Restorative justice brings victims and offenders of crime face to face to collectively resolve conflict and repair the harm caused by an offence in a way that is respectful to both parties.[1] Over the past twenty-five years, it has emerged as a popular social movement in criminal justice. As a way of dealing with conflict, however, it was long practised by some indigenous cultures before the advent of Western-style criminal justice systems (Braithwaite, 2002).

A widely accepted definition among practitioners and academics characterizes restorative justice as 'a process whereby the parties with a stake in a particular offense come together to resolve collectively how to deal with the aftermath of the offense and its implications for the future' (Marshall, 1999). The format and language may vary, but the common aim of restorative justice is to offer an alternative to the formal adversarial justice system so that families and communities can play a direct role in creating their own justice.

Since the 1970s, there has been steadily growing interest in establishing restorative justice as a complement, or alternative, to Western-style justice systems (Immarigeon and Daly, 1997). This has been primarily due to community, victim, and offender disillusionment with the criminal justice system. Its uptake has also been influenced by economic considerations such as the rising cost of punitive sanctions, a desire of governments and individuals to implement informal and indigenous processes whenever possible, and society's embrace of alternative dispute resolution in response to interpersonal conflict.

Mediation practitioners, faith communities, and formal criminal justice institutions have implemented a variety of restorative justice programmes. The dominant models worldwide include victim-offender mediation (also known as victim-offender reconciliation programmes), restitution programmes, sentencing circles, and family group conferencing programmes (also known as restorative justice conferencing). Variations in programmes arise from their

---

[1] I agree with Cook's statement that the terms 'victim' and 'offender', while potentially stigmatizing, are a necessary analytic shorthand and I will use those terms throughout this book (Cook, 2006).

diverse national origins. Victim-offender mediation, victim-offender reconciliation, and sentencing circle programmes originated in North America—predominately through the efforts of Mennonite and Quaker communities as well as the Canadian and Navajo First Nation Aboriginals (Taylor Griffiths and Hamilton, 1996; Yazzie and Zion, 1996). Family group conferencing (or restorative justice conferencing) emerged mainly in New Zealand from Maori traditions of sanctioning and dispute resolution (Pratt, 1996).

This book will focus on restorative justice conferences—a popular delivery of restorative justice in the UK, Northern Ireland, Australia, and New Zealand. Sherman and Strang (2012) have suggested that the increasing popularity of restorative justice conferences indicates that the movement is on the verge of a 'tipping point' of mainstream adoption in common law countries. They define a restorative justice conference by three elements (Sherman and Strang, 2012: 220):

1. The presence in one room at the same time of one or more victims, the victims' offender(s) who accept(s) responsibility (if not legal guilt) for a crime, the respective friends or families of victims and offenders, and a facilitator to guide their discussion;
2. The provision of enough time for everyone present (including the offender) to express their emotions about the crime and the harm it has caused, as well as to suggest what should be done about it;
3. The facilitator's effort to reach a conclusion that expresses a group consensus about what the offender should do to address some of the issues raised by participants.

The United States, New Zealand, and Canadian Departments of Justice and the United Kingdom Ministry of Justice have all developed 'best practice' guidelines for restorative justice (Home Office, 2003; Hughes and Mossman, 2001; New Zealand Ministry of Justice, 2004). In Australia, every state and territory includes restorative justice principles in their criminal or juvenile justice legislation. In the UK, the Youth Justice Boards of England and Wales have made restorative principles an explicit aspect of their policy of dealing with youth crime (Home Office, 2003) and an amendment to the Crime and Courts Bill, proposed in 2012, introduced a legislative basis for restorative justice for adults, proposing to give courts the power to defer sentencing until a conference takes place.[2]

---

[2] Crime and Courts Bill (2012–13), sched 15(2).

The UK Ministry of Justice, in collaboration with the Restorative Justice Council, has also established the first ever register of restorative justice to connect victims and offenders to practitioners,[3] leading to increasing awareness and support of this practice. The US Department of Justice held a symposium on restorative justice in 2000, producing recommendations for local government policies (Bilchick, 1998) and United Nations affiliates have conducted a review of programmes worldwide with suggestions and endorsement for their future uptake (Tkachuk, 2002).

In sum, the restorative justice movement is gaining public and legislative support throughout the world and its supporters hope to ensure these practices make an important contribution to the criminal justice system (Lee, 1996; Pranis and Umbreit, 1992; Shapland et al, 2006). However, there are still many unanswered questions about the effectiveness of the process because, in spite of many evaluations, it is still not known when, and for whom, restorative justice works best. As we shall see, without a way to measure whether a restorative justice conference is successful on the micro level, it is not possible to accurately judge its effectiveness.

Defining Success in Restorative Justice

Criminologists have long been arguing over the key aims of restorative justice (Daly, 2001; Hoyle, Young, and Hill, 2002; Robinson and Shapland, 2008). A first approach suggests that reduced recidivism is a clear goal of many government supported restorative justice schemes. A second approach focuses on outcomes for participants other than the offender, particularly victims and communities (Braithwaite, 2002; Robinson and Shapland, 2008). A third approach, which informs this analysis, emphasizes process rather than outcomes, whether for the offender or other participants. It evaluates the success of a conference as a justice ritual, focusing on immediate positive outcomes such as group solidarity and cohesion. These different definitions of success can be combined, such as when sociologists of emotion consider the relationship between short-term emotions and long-term emotional states and behavioural outcomes (Collins, 1990, 2004). Indeed, Chapter Seven of this book will show the link between ritually successful restorative

---

[3] See <http://www.restorativejustice.org.uk/register>

justice conferences and offending behaviour. Through a careful analysis of qualitative and quantitative data, I will argue that moving to a micro level view of restorative justice interactions can provide us with a rigorous framework through which to evaluate its success.

Restorative justice has been cited as an example of a process that brings emotion to a justice system that has been traditionally based on rationality and classical deterrence (Sherman, 2003). The astute reader will note the double meaning in the title for this book. Are emotions driving 'just' outcomes? Or is it more than just emotions? How does the 'emotionality' of restorative justice translate to successful justice outcomes? The expression of emotions plays a very important role in restorative justice conferences but, in order for these emotions to have an impact on the success of a conference, they need to be carefully managed and utilized to create powerful rituals.

Outline of this Book

The research presented in this book examines if, and how, a restorative justice conference can be a transformative event for offenders and victims, with the potential to reduce offending. I will argue that the emotional and ritual dynamics within a restorative justice conference hold the key to understanding, monitoring, and measuring its success.

Traditional theories of restorative justice focus on the content of the interaction and its ability to incite specific emotions such as shame (Braithwaite, 1989; Retzinger and Scheff, 1996) or activate feelings of trust and legitimacy (Sherman, 1993; Tyler, 1990). I suggest that, beyond the content of the interaction, it is the dynamic process of building rhythm and a shared focus over time in the conference that culminates in expressions of group solidarity. It is this solidarity that is translated into long-term emotional well-being and the potential for reduced offending. A review of the current research and theory on the role of emotions in restorative justice is presented in Chapter Two.

In Chapter Three, I suggest that we can develop a deeper understanding of how restorative justice works if we conceive of it as a justice ritual, and focus our attention on the micro level processes that vary from conference to conference. Using Collins's (2004) theory of interaction ritual chains, I emphasize how collective emotion and solidarity is produced through the course of such a justice ritual. This chapter also describes in more detail the data and methodologies used in this book.

In Chapter Four, I examine in detail a case study of a single conference run by the Metropolitan Police. A video recording of a conference between a man pleading guilty of robbery and his victim is used to show the micro processes through which rhythm and entrainment develop over time. I explore the role of turning points and the way participants' linguistic and paralinguistic cues can alter the emotional dynamics in the group. I also examine how conferences can develop as power and status rituals, and the impact these imbalances of power have on the participants. Close analysis of this case identifies some of the key features of a conference, which are further examined in subsequent chapters.

Chapter Five uses qualitative interviews with restorative justice facilitators and offenders from the London restorative justice study to explore the components of interaction ritual in subjectively defined 'successful' and 'unsuccessful' conferences. I will show how facilitators prepare participants to maximize their emotions and follow turn-taking rules, and how they use a set of strategies to engage participants in conversational rhythm and balance. I will identify key emotional 'turning points'—specific moments where the rhythm changes from one of conflict to one of solidarity. Exploring how interaction ritual can fail in 'unsuccessful' conferences is particularly useful for further illuminating the micro processes of a successful interaction. As such, this analysis also includes conferences that did not achieve positive short-term outcomes such as solidarity or emotional energy.

Chapter Six further explores the concepts of solidarity and other short-term outcomes, using data from interviews with facilitators to examine the elements of successful and unsuccessful restorative justice rituals. Having explored the elements of interaction ritual in the preparatory and beginning stages of the conference, and the short-term ritual outcomes, this chapter will then shift focus to use some of the key concepts identified in the qualitative research to quantitatively test for the elements of interaction ritual in systematic observations of restorative justice conferences. Using systematic observations of conferences in Canberra, Australia, from the landmark Reintegrative Shaming Experiments ('RISE') study of restorative justice (Sherman, Strang, and Woods, 2000),

I statistically examine the structure of a restorative justice conference and develop measures for key interaction ritual variables such as conversational balance, solidarity, and emotional energy. I conduct an empirical test of interaction ritual theory, using systematic observations of conferences, to propose an empirical model to determine whether ritual ingredients actually do produce ritual outcomes in the short-term. By analysing the elements of these interactions I find evidence that one can predict short-term success such as group solidarity.

In Chapter Seven, I move to an analysis of reoffending, using systematic observations of conferences from the RISE study (Sherman, Strang, and Woods, 2000) to examine the long-term effects of interaction ritual, testing whether ritually successful conferences are more likely to reduce offending than less successful conferences. I show how situational and ritual aspects of a conference are key components of any crime reduction effects. The results of this analysis show that, controlling for other situational and individual characteristics, high solidarity conferences will result in significantly less offending than low solidarity conferences up to five years after a restorative justice interaction. I also return to the qualitative data to explore the long-term emotional well-being of offenders who have participated in restorative justice.

Taken together, this research emphasizes the micro components of restorative justice as the key to understanding its potential as an emotionally powerful and transformative event. The findings contribute to theory and research on micro interaction and restorative justice and I conclude by sketching the outline for a theory of restorative justice. I present the implications of this work for criminal justice policy and practice and provide useful policy-friendly steps to ensure the potential of restorative justice is actually achieved in practice.

This research provides input into what we know about how emotions and interactions work at a group level as well as a contribution to the development of a theoretical framework for the restorative justice movement. I use a variety of perspectives to address my research questions and employ multiple methods such as qualitative interviews; micro observations of discourse, face, and demeanour; and quantitative analysis of systematic observations of conferences. I also show how we can observe, measure, and analyse the micro dynamics and structure of a conference. It is hoped that this multimethod approach to addressing interaction ritual in restorative justice will paint a complete picture of the conference process and, ultimately, lead to a better understanding of restorative justice.

2

The Promise of Emotional Transformation

My first experience with restorative justice was while working as a researcher with the Metropolitan Police in the London study of restorative justice for serious adult offenders.[1] One of my duties was to support the police facilitators as they organized and ran their conferences. While a particular facilitator was ultimately responsible for running a conference, in reality its organization was often a group effort. Facilitators brainstormed together about how to approach complex cases, sought each other's advice when they hit stumbling blocks, and debriefed afterwards about what worked and what didn't. When a facilitator returned to the office after a conference, their colleagues gathered around them, eager to hear about what had happened. Over cups of tea the facilitator described the details, unexpected events, high and low points, etc. If they were pleased with a conference, they often said something like, 'It was great! Real emotional!', and the other facilitators would nod in understanding. There was an implicit acceptance about what 'emotional' meant, and that it was a good thing. Further elaboration was seldom necessary.

It was widely accepted by these facilitators that 'emotional' meant good and 'flat' meant bad. This is consistent with the larger rhetoric among practitioners and scholars that emotions are at the heart of restorative justice. It is often lauded as an 'emotionally intelligent' approach to dealing with victims and offenders (Sherman, 2003; King, 2008). Restorative justice is portrayed as a uniquely emotional encounter in a way that other criminal justice interactions cannot, and perhaps should not, be. What is driving this? What do people really mean when they talk about emotions and restorative justice? What makes emotions good, and why?

---

[1] It is from this study that I draw a large amount of the data analysed in this book.

There are many claims about the promise of restorative justice. It has been suggested it can repair harm to victims and communities, restore and reintegrate offenders, and reduce reoffending. Common to these claims is the idea that 'emotions' are driving its potential success. This is the big promise of restorative justice— that somehow an emotional transformation will take place to heal victims and turn offenders into law-abiding citizens.

This chapter will explore what we know about emotions and restorative justice. I will examine some of the leading theories that explain the role of emotions and their potential to repair harm and reduce offending. I will argue that these theories do not go far enough and that, by introducing a micro sociological perspective informed by theories of ritual, we can begin to understand how emotions work in the complex and dynamic interactions that make up restorative justice conferences.

Claims of Restorative Justice

Restorative justice has been offered as an antidote to all that ails criminal justice. It has been pregnant with promise since its inception. Common claims include its inherent fairness and legitimacy, its potential to heal victims of their trauma, and its ability to reduce reoffending. These claims are outlined below.[2]

A fair, satisfying, and legitimate process for victims and offenders

Most of the research suggests that offenders and victims perceive restorative justice as being fairer than court. Interviews with offenders reveal they are more likely to understand what is going on in a conference and to feel more empowered and respected (Barnes, 1999; Sherman and Barnes, 1997). Sherman and Barnes also found that offenders have an increased respect for police officers and the law after attending a conference.

Umbreit and colleagues (Umbreit, 1998; Umbreit and Coates, 1993; Umbreit, Coates, and Kalanj, 1994; Umbreit, Coates, and

---

[2] There are many other claims such as the potential to heal communities and promote democracy and non-domination. The three listed above appear the most frequently and will be explored with the methods used in this book. See Braithwaite (2002) and Sherman and Strang (2007) for a full review.

Roberts, 2000) found high levels of satisfaction and perceived legitimacy both for victims and offenders in their interviews with participants in restorative justice programmes in the United States and the UK. In their analyses, restorative justice (compared to a non-randomized comparison group) contributed to higher rates of victim and offender satisfaction, higher frequency—and larger amounts—of restitution paid to victims, and a reduction of fear and anxiety for the victims. Many of these results were replicated in New Zealand where victims were much more likely to receive repara- tion and offenders and victims both had higher levels of satisfac- tion following a conference (Morris and Maxwell, 1998; Morris, Maxwell, and Robertson, 1993). Additionally, in other studies, victims were found to be more satisfied when they felt mediation provided a greater understanding of the crime as well as an oppor- tunity to express their feelings (Coates and Gehm, 1989; Evje and Cushman, 2000). Finally, in a comprehensive study of restorative justice for offenders in the UK, it was found that the large majority of victims and offenders found their conferences to be useful, felt a sense of closure, and were more satisfied with their procedures than those who went to court (Shapland et al, 2007). Notably, those whose offences were most serious were significantly more likely to find their conference useful compared with those whose offences were less serious.

Victim and offender satisfaction has also been found to be related to a perception that the restorative justice conference process is fair and inclusive (Strang, 2002). Evaluation of restorative justice in New Zealand reported that a minority of victims and offend- ers felt worse after a conference, specifically when they reported not being involved in reaching an outcome (Morris and Maxwell, 1993; Morris, Maxwell, and Robertson, 1993). Nevertheless, they stressed that young people were more likely to feel involved in their conference than when they went through the court system (Morris and Maxwell, 1993). This complements Strang and Sherman's (1997) finding that a small number of victims were dissatisfied after a conference and felt disrespected because of something that was said. Similarly, Shapland and colleagues found that the minority of participants that were unhappy with their conference pointed to instances where they felt they were not being taken seriously, or felt uninformed or not included in follow-up after the conference (Shapland et al, 2007). Finally, Choi and colleagues pointed out that when victims are unhappy with their experience of restorative justice it is often when they feel little attention has been paid to the process and most of the focus has been on developing suitable outcomes for the offender (Choi et al, 2012). Although such cases are greatly outnumbered by those with positive outcomes, they do highlight the links between the process of restorative justice and subsequent satisfaction. Not all conferences are 'good' conferences, and when elements of the process go wrong, participants can feel worse than they did prior to the interaction.

A healing process for victims

There is clear evidence that restorative justice is beneficial to victims of crime. Symbolic reparation, generally in the form of an apology, is often most important to victims' satisfaction levels (Strang and Sherman, 1997; Strang, 2002). Victims who meet their offender and receive an apology are, more often than not, more forgiving, feel more sympathetic towards the offender, and are less likely to desire physical revenge (Sherman and Strang, 2007). Similarly, Poulson's (2003) review of studies illustrates a range of positive psychological outcomes for both victims and offenders.

Randomized trials in the UK, which built on Strang's (2002) work, provided conclusive evidence of increased well-being for victims who meet with their offender (Sherman et al, 2005; Strang and Sherman, 2004). This was confirmed by Angel (2005) who measured Post Traumatic Stress ('PTS') symptoms in victims of crime in experimental and control groups in London and found significantly reduced levels of PTS symptoms both immediately following a conference and at a six-month follow-up.

Reducing reoffending

The evidence is mixed on the deterrent effect of restorative justice and better tests are required to measure and monitor reoffending outcomes. We know, for example, that it reduces offending in some cases, increases it in others, and has no effect in still others. There is also evidence of a type of secondary deterrence—namely a reduced desire for revenge by victims, which prevents future crime (Sherman and Strang, 2011). Unfortunately, due to the many challenges of adequate implementation and evaluation, much research on restorative justice and recidivism has been hindered by the lack of an adequate comparison group, insufficient statistical power, or other methodological issues. The most rigorous evaluations of restorative justice employ either a randomized or matched control group for comparison which, although few in number, suggest the potential for restorative justice as a crime reduction strategy.

McGarrell and Hipple used a randomized control group to evaluate restorative justice and recidivism in Indiana (McGarrell, 2000; McGarrell and Hipple, 2007). At the one and two year follow-up they found that the rates of recidivism in juveniles who participated in a conference were much lower than in the control group. They also used survival analysis to show that conference offenders had a slower failure rate than the control group. However, they also revealed that the positive effect of restorative justice one year after the conference was greater than at two years, which suggests a decay in effectiveness over time. Luke and Lind (2002) obtained similar results for juvenile offenders using similar methods with different data from Australia. While Jones (2009) did not employ a control group, he used propensity score matching to compare adult offenders who participated in a conference with similar adult offenders in the magistrates' courts in New South Wales, Australia. He found no significant differences in reoffending behaviour between the two groups.[3]

Meta-analysis of randomized and matched control evaluations of restorative justice also suggests its potential crime reduction effects. Bradshaw and Roseborough (2005) evaluated a number of studies to show that restorative justice contributed to a twenty-six per cent reduction in recidivism, which represented significantly less offending compared with the control groups. Latimer, Dowden, and Muise (2005) also employed meta-analysis to find a similar reduction in recidivism, although their evidence was tempered by self-selection into restorative justice. In a comprehensive review of the experiments, or high quality quasi-experimental evaluations of restorative justice, Sherman and Strang (2007) concluded that on average offenders who have a restorative justice conference commit

---

[3] See also De Beus and Rodriguez (2007); Luke and Lind (2002); Maxwell and Morris (2001); McCold and Wachtel (1998); Nugent, Williams, and Umbreit (2004); Rodriguez (2007); Triggs (2005); Umbreit (1998); Umbreit, Coates, and Roberts (2000); and Schneider (1986). Using a combination of experimental and quasi-experimental techniques, these researchers also found reduced levels of offending through restorative justice to varying degrees of statistical and substantive significance.

fewer offences than those who do not. This is particularly true for offenders who commit violent crimes.

Perhaps the most comprehensive experiment to date examined the effect of restorative justice in violent, property, and drink-driving conferences as a diversion from prosecution (Sherman, Strang, and Woods, 2000). The major findings were a large and significant drop in offending rates by violent offenders, an increase in offending by those arrested for drink-driving, and no perceptible change in offending for juvenile property offenders. Re-analysis of the data found that while reoffending might be somewhat reduced among white Australians, the process may have an adverse impact on indigenous Australians (Sherman, Strang, and Woods, 2004). Indigenous offenders who participated in a conference which was generally organized by a white police officer and involved white victims were significantly more likely to reoffend compared to the control group. The non-indigenous sample had similar, or slightly lower, offending patterns compared to the control group, which suggests that the dynamics of the conferences were different for these two groups.

This evidence suggests that individual characteristics, such as ethnicity, as well as features of the conference itself may influence how people respond to it. While not intended as an analysis of reoffending, Cook (2006) used qualitative data to explore how the performance of gender and race was connected to power dynamics and notions of accountability in restorative justice conferences. Her research hinted at wide micro level variations in the dynamics of conferences that may influence reoffending outcomes.

Hayes and Daly's notable effort to systematically examine the effects of variations within conferences looked at how specific dynamics of the conference (in addition to individual character-istics) are associated with future offending. Using observations of juvenile conferences in Adelaide, South Australia, they found that offending was less likely when offenders were remorseful *and* the outcome agreement was decided by general consensus (Hayes and Daly, 2003). This important finding suggests that examining the dynamics of conferences in-depth is more productive than doing more generalized comparisons with courts. Using different data Hayes and Daly later found that individual characteristics such as age, gender, and prior offending history influenced post-conference behaviour, but features of the conference (as judged by offenders immediately after the conference) did not have any significant association with post-conference offending behaviour (Hayes and Daly, 2004). However, these were not objective measures of conference features and the data was also collected as the participants were finishing the conference. Subsequently, almost all offenders gave high ratings on all items in their survey.

Similarly, in an evaluation of a large experiment in restorative justice, Shapland and colleagues found a significant relationship between offenders' views about the conference, observers' views about the conference, and reoffending (Shapland et al, 2008). They found that a decrease in offending was associated with offenders who: felt that the conference helped them realize the harm they had caused, wanted to meet the victim, and were observed to be actively participating in the conference.

Such research implies that an understanding of interactional and emotional dynamics of the conference may be the key to understanding how it influences future offending. This seems like a step in the right direction to understanding the emotional dynamics of conferences but more work needs to be done in this area.[4] Careful examination of what people actually do and say in conferences can reveal key features of how emotions work.

How Emotions Work in Restorative Encounters

There tends to be an assumption that the reason restorative justice can achieve all these promises is because it is 'emotionally intelligent'—it can somehow harness all the good emotions while dispelling the bad ones, restore broken bonds, and reintegrate offenders. How does this happen? A number of theories have been used to account for how emotions work in these encounters. Briefly, I will review the key theories around shame, legitimacy, and related emotions. I will suggest that while specific emotions may be evoked

---

[4] Morris and Maxwell (1993) used offender interviews to look at features of the conference. They found that offenders who perceived the process to be more respectful and inclusive were less likely to commit future offences. Statistical tests were not conducted, however, and the author can only infer that procedural differences between cases contributed to offending differentials. Additional analysis showed that conference factors such as the offender feeling remorseful; feeling involved; agreeing with the outcomes; and apologizing to the victim were related to reductions in reoffending (Maxwell and Morris, 2001). A potential problem with this research with juvenile offenders was that the data was collected in interviews conducted six to seven years after their conferences.

in restorative justice encounters, and that these emotions may be important in bringing about positive change, we need to develop a better understanding of the micro level dynamics of the interaction to fully understand how these emotions work in restorative justice.

Shame and related emotions

Shame is a slippery concept. As Harris and Maruna (2008) rightly note, the best analysis of what shame is, and how it works in our everyday lives is more likely to be found in poetry, literature, and art than in academic writing. The story of shame in restorative justice is long and complex. It has consistently been the most discussed and written about concept. Below, I will briefly summarize the major debates about shame and other moral emotions in restorative justice. As this is an evolving discussion with many complexities and side issues, I will organize this discussion as a type of social history of how the concept of shame has been used to account for some of the claims of restorative justice.

Early conceptions of shame in restorative justice

Early work on shame includes theories about the act of shaming and the actual feeling of shame. Of course, this all started with Braithwaite's now classic distinction between stigmatic and reintegrative shaming (Braithwaite, 1989). When first laying out the tenets of reintegrative shaming theory, Braithwaite imaginatively, and convincingly, argued that most criminal justice processes and sanctions shame an offender in a way that is stigmatizing—condemning not just the wrongdoing but the individual themselves.

Reintegrative shaming, on the other hand, is a respectful process where disapproval of the criminal act is expressed but offenders are given a chance to express remorse and can then be welcomed back into the community. While stigmatizing shaming can have long-term negative impacts on an individual, reintegrative shaming is likely to strengthen social bonds and internally build a conscience that prevents future wrongdoing. This theory has been widely used by academics and practitioners to account for the claims of restorative justice. While shame plays a central role in this theory, there is little discussion of what this emotion actually is and how it works (Harris and Maruna, 2008).

Other scholars shift the focus from the external act of shaming to the internal process of *feeling* ashamed. Social psychologists Scheff and Retzinger argued that shame is repressed in contemporary society, and 'shameful' emotions, rather than being openly acknowledged in everyday interaction, are often 'bypassed' (Scheff and Retzinger, 1991). This can have pathological consequences where an individual becomes stuck in a 'feeling trap'—that is, they feel shame which leads to repression or unacknowledgement, which in turn leads to further shame about the original shame. The results of this feeling trap may be anger, rage, or even violence. Over time, unacknowledged shame can lead to dysfunctional patterns of communication.

Retzinger and Scheff (1996) further argued that this can be avoided if shame is acknowledged in a productive way. A restorative justice conference, for example, can bring shame to the surface in a way that redirects aggressive emotions and leads to empathy and pride. When an offender acknowledges the shame of their act and the victim acknowledges the shame of their victimization, the two can come to some sort of symbolic reparation and reintegration, usually through the expression of remorse and forgiveness. As with Braithwaite's work on shame and social bonds, however, Retzinger and Scheff did not explain the mechanism that allow expressed shame to become a reintegrative experience.

The plot thickens: the many faces of shame and related emotions

While the central importance of shame has been largely accepted in the restorative justice community, a number of alternative explanations have been suggested. At the same time, empirical work on the role of shame has challenged some of the initial assumptions.

In particular, guilt, remorse, and empathy are commonly evoked as alternative emotions to explain 'how restorative justice works' (Van Stokkom, 2002; Harris, Walgrave, and Braithwaite, 2004). Van Stokkom drew on the work of Tangney to argue that guilt is a more productive emotion in restorative justice conferences than shame. Tangney's work showed that guilt, unlike shame which leads to negative feelings about the self, focuses on negative feelings about the act, leaving the self intact (Tangney, 1995). She also found a relationship between feelings of guilt and a sense of empathy. In a restorative justice context, Tangney's work suggested that expressions of guilt allowed both the offender and victim to develop a shared empathy, leading to forgiveness and a repaired social bond. However, Tangney did not distinguish between stigmatic and reintegrative shame, or acknowledged and bypassed shame, and taking these distinctions into account may change her empirical conclusions. Furthermore, Harris, Walgrave, and Braithwaite (2004) argued that it is theoretically and empirically difficult to distinguish shame from these other emotions, and that guilt, remorse, and empathy are likely to spill over into feelings of shame.

Empirical work in restorative justice shows that shame plays a major role, but not necessarily in the way theorized by Braithwaite (Harris, 2001, 2003; Harris, Walgrave, and Braithwaite, 2004). The real story is much more complex. In Harris's (2001) analysis of surveys and systematic observations of conferences and court he identified three distinct dimensions of shame-related emotions among participants: shame-guilt, embarrassment-exposure, and unresolved shame. Shame-guilt is characterized by feelings of having done wrong, concern for others, feeling ashamed and angry at oneself, and loss of honour. Harris (2003) concluded that the distinctions between shame and guilt are overtheorized, and that they fall into similar categories for those who experience them. Embarrassment-exposure is a separate dimension of shame, encompassing a feeling of being exposed or on display. Similar to Scheff and Retzinger's conception of unacknowledged shame, unresolved shame is related to ongoing feelings that issues were not resolved in the restorative justice conference. Additionally, while early forms of reintegrative shaming theory conceptualized shame and reintegration as steps along a continuum, Harris's work suggested that shaming, stigmatizing, and reintegrative acts can happen simultaneously in restorative justice conferences and that the difficulty in capturing a single dimension or experience of shame belies how complex this emotion is.

There is an implicit assumption that shaming causes shame. However, as Walgrave and Aertsten (1996) have noted, one is likely to follow the other only when the relationship between the shame inducer and the person shamed is believed to be legitimate and meaningful. Otherwise, acts of shaming constitute empty rhetoric that will be largely disregarded by an offender. Using this hypothesis, Harris tested whether the practices of shaming, stigmatization, or reintegration actually do produce emotions of shame (characterized by the three dimensions of shame he previously developed). He found that shame-guilt was predicted by a perception of having been reintegrated and not being stigmatized, while embarrassment-exposure and unresolved shame were predicted by perceptions of stigmatization.

Reconceptions: shame, shaming, and shame management

In response to many of the issues raised above, Braithwaite and Braithwaite (2001) reformulated reintegrative shaming theory by laying out thirty propositions that explicitly linked shame, pride, stigmatization, reintegration, and restorative justice. Specifically, they acknowledged Braithwaite's earlier work as undertheorizing the relationship between shaming behaviour and the resulting emotions of shame and pride. Incorporating elements of unacknowledged shame theory, they argued that in addition to making sure conferences are reintegrative and not stigmatic, one must bring shame to the surface in a positive way and not allow it to be bypassed. This laid the way for recent work on shame theory that puts more of an emphasis on shame management, whereby people are encouraged to acknowledge shame and cultivate pride (Harris and Maruna, 2006; Ahmed et al, 2001).

Legitimacy and procedural justice

While much of the debate around shame focuses on unpacking the dimensions of specific emotions, other theories that account for the claims made in restorative justice focus on the procedural aspects of the restorative justice encounter. In procedural justice theory (Tyler and Huo, 2002; Tyler, 1990), for example, participants' attitudes and their perceptions of the fairness and legitimacy of the restorative justice process are evaluated and analysed. Tyler and Huo (2002) have suggested that we come to believe in the authority of the police and justice system when we believe that the justice process is legitimate and trustworthy. Thus, in offering a progressive alternative to mainstream justice, restorative justice builds legitimacy because its procedures are believed to be fair. Theoretically at least, and in contrast to the court, which is impersonal and strictly hierarchical, restorative justice conferences are voluntary—the structure is fair and democratic and they are run by the participants (with the guidance of a facilitator). Furthermore, Doak and O'Mahony (2011) suggested that restorative justice conferencing for juveniles has the capacity to build legitimacy in state actors and, perhaps more importantly, between different sections of communities—in their example, Unionist and Nationalist communities in Northern Ireland.

Sherman's defiance theory, which is based on many of the same assumptions as procedural justice theory, argued that similar criminal sanctions have different effects for offenders in different social situations (Sherman, 1993). Defiance occurs when an offender views a sanction as illegitimate; has weak bonds to the sanctioning agent; or denies his, or her, shame in the offence. Deterrence, on the other hand, can be effected if the sanctions are regarded as legitimate; offenders express shame for their actions; and they have strong bonds with mainstream society. Sherman suggested that appearing in court is more likely to produce defiance while the restorative conference is more likely to promote deterrence.

This is consistent with the many studies that show that offenders and victims are more satisfied with restorative justice compared to court. As Tyler's theory suggested, these increased levels of perceived fairness and legitimacy may be why some offenders who participate in restorative conferences subsequently show increased compliance with the law (Tyler, 1990).

What We Do and Don't Know About Emotions

The common thread in these theories is that they place emotion at the centre of the justice process—an element often missing from criminological theory (Karstedt, 2002; Sherman, 2003). Although the literature provides compelling evidence that restorative justice is indeed reintegrative, and may reduce offending, there is really very little in-depth analysis of how this happens. I suggest that current theories of how restorative justice works are missing an important component. Specifically, they look at the content of the conference, that is, what was said, how people felt, how ashamed a person was, and how much respect they were given. By focusing on the content, however, they ignore the process and dynamics of the conference, which include how rhythms and emotions are developed and sustained over time. This may be, in part, a methodological deficiency—it is a challenge to systematically collect data on such things. But, without in-depth analyses of conferences themselves—both those that serve the reintegrative function well and those that do not—one cannot observe or measure the rich array of social process and contextual factors that might influence conferencing outcomes.

The idea that 'restorative justice is good because it allows participants to express their emotions' does not adequately explain the phenomena. There is more to the story. Specifically, I argue that we need to look beyond emotions to the micro structure of the interaction. In Chapter Three I propose a framework through which we can analyse restorative justice conferences by examining the structure and process of a conference as a ritual. I will argue that success in restorative justice means ritual success, where the participants are emotionally transformed over the course of the interaction. This emotional transformation can be a fleeting sense of empathy or bonding, or perhaps it can impact behaviour long after the conference has ended.

3

The Ritual Elements

Rituals in the Justice Process

The research on restorative justice has shown that conferences can be transformative, producing high levels of satisfaction and even a commitment to stop offending. They can also fall flat, with little emotional investment or return for the participants. The theories reviewed in Chapter Two suggested that one reason conferences succeed is because they bring about the 'good kind' of shame as opposed to the 'harmful kind'. That is, the non-hierarchical and participatory nature of the conference instils a sense of legitimacy into the proceedings, leading victims and offenders to believe the criminal justice system is just and fair. While all of this may be true, it is not clear on a micro level how these interactions work to produce the 'right kind' of shame, or enable participants to feel they have a say or are empowered. Indeed, numerous scholars have called for an in-depth investigation of the processes and dynamics of conferences (Braithwaite, 2002; Braithwaite, Ahmed, and Braithwaite, 2006; Hayes and Daly, 2003). In order to do that, we need a framework to orient ourselves.

A useful way to think of the processes and dynamics of restorative justice is as a kind of ritual. The concept of justice as a ritual has always been a component of both scholarly writing and the public imagination (Foucault, 1977; Garland, 1993; Maruna, 2011). Rituals are important because of the sense of collective solidarity they engender. In sociology, this line of thinking originates with Durkheim, who demonstrated how, by bringing people together with a common cause, rituals are an important part of community building and help create a sense of togetherness. In his study of religion (Durkheim, 1912), Durkheim suggested that the reason people engage in such rituals is because of the resulting feeling of 'collective effervescence', or ecstatic energy, and a feeling of group membership. At the height of such a ritual, participants feel swept away, transformed, and at one with the group. As Durkheim described,

> It seems to him that he has become a new being…and because his companions feel transformed in the same way at the same moment, and express this feeling by their shouts, movements, and bearings, it is as if he was in reality transported into a special world entirely different from the one in which he ordinarily lives, a special world inhabited by exceptionally intense forces that invade and transform him. (Durkheim, 1912: 220.)

It is this search for collective effervescence that keeps us coming back to participate in rituals like religious ceremonies.

Karstedt (2006) argued that justice rituals are important because of their potential to transform one emotion into another, for example where negative feelings of anger, fear, or humiliation may be transformed through a positive ritual into feelings of solidarity and shared morality. Schechner (1981) suggested that rituals may go further than transforming emotions and can even transform the self. He distinguished between transportative and transformative rituals, specifically in performed rituals (be it theatre, or 'rites of passage'). Transportative rituals can take us to a different place while we are performing in the ritual, but once it's over we return to the everyday life we had been living. Transformative rituals, on the other hand, actually change who we are. Schechner's idea of a performative ritual is apt—dramaturgical metaphors are rife in restorative justice theory and practice. The facilitator follows a 'script' to make sure all participants play their 'role'. Powerful performers are referred to as 'stars', while failed conferences are 'duds'. Restorative justice performances/rituals toe the line between transportative and transformative. As Karstedt pointed out, such rituals aim to transform negative emotions into positive ones. While the other participants/co-performers can be transported and swept up in the collective effervescence, there is the hope that the offender will be transformed. In this way then, the restorative justice ritual can engender more than a collective pleasant emotion of group membership—it can create moral beings.

Based on this, we can conclude that not only do rituals create and reaffirm a sense of group membership, they are actually the *source* of morality and public order. For example, Durkheim argued that public rituals in response to a crime or misbehaviour serve to bind a community together, both through the formal spectacle of punishment and the informal rituals of people getting together to gossip about the offender and the punishment imposed. Through the enactment and re-enactment of justice rituals, we come to a shared moral standard of right and wrong. This has important implications for reintegrative shaming theory. As Braithwaite argued, reintegrative shaming works to stop reoffending not just because we want to avoid future instances of shame. Rather, it is through such shaming that we develop a 'learned conscience' and a new set of morals (Braithwaite, 1989: 37). The Durkheimian tradition in sociology would suggest that this happens because reintegrative shaming can be a community-building, transformative ritual.

Goffman (1967) extended this insight to show that solidarity-creating rituals do not only occur in formal rituals (such as religious ceremonies) but appear in all facets of everyday life. He shifted the focus of attention away from the individual, and what they are feeling, to the encounter as the unit of analysis, examining every interaction for its ritual elements. This way, we come to see how our sense of who we are and what we mean to other people is constantly negotiated through interaction rituals, be it a chat with an acquaintance whom we meet on the street, a paper we give at an academic conference, or an intimate conversation with a loved one.

Goffman is particularly adept at showing what happens when rituals fail. Interaction rituals can break down for a number of reasons: a participant can fail to respond appropriately, or may offend other participants, become distracted, misunderstand what is happening, or lose face in some other way. When this happens, they feel the opposite of solidarity—perhaps awkward, uninterested, or even repelled by the experience. However, neither Durkheim nor Goffman specified the conditions under which rituals are likely to succeed and fail. Partly in response to this, Collins (2004) has developed a theory of 'interaction ritual chains' which provides a set of principles for predicting when an interaction will work and make us feel good, or fail and make us feel bad. Over time, these repeated chains of ritualistic social interactions raise or lower feelings of long-term social bonding, motivation towards social goals, and commitment to group symbols and shared morality.

Collins conceived of social interaction as a series of rituals that build on each other to provide an individual with varying levels of positive or negative emotional energy. He identified four main ingredients for a successful ritual: group assembly, a barrier to outsiders, mutual focus, and a shared mood.

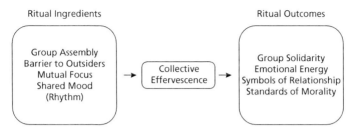

Ritual Ingredients   Ritual Outcomes

Group Assembly
Barrier to Outsiders   Group Solidarity
Mutual Focus   Collective   Emotional Energy
Shared Mood   Effervescence   Symbols of Relationship
(Rhythm)   Standards of Morality

Figure 3.1 Interaction Ritual Model (modified from Collins 2004)

A key feature of this model is whether a threshold or take-off point is reached, after which these elements feed back upon each other and lead the group to develop rhythmic coordination and synchronization in their conversation, bodily movements, and emotions. When participants become 'caught up in the rhythm and mood of the talk' (Collins, 2004: 48), the collective effervescence Durkheim predicted in formal religious ceremonies can occur in any social interaction. The outcomes of successful interaction rituals, therefore, are group solidarity and emotional energy, a development or evocation of symbols that represent the social relationship, and the emergence of group standards of morality. These outcomes will be explored below.

Collins's theory lends itself well to understanding the process of restorative justice. A powerful justice ritual that brings about feelings of group membership, solidarity, and a shared morality can certainly be considered a successful reintegration ceremony (Braithwaite and Mugford, 1994; Maruna, 2011).

The language of ritual has long been used to describe restorative justice encounters. In an early treatise on restorative approaches to justice, Zehr (1990) uses Pfhol's (1981) idea of a 'ritual or reordering' to describe restorative justice events. Such rituals can reset a wrong and bring an individual to the place he or she was before the commission of an offence. With a nod to Durkheim, Zehr noted that perhaps churches are the best places to organize such rituals (Zehr, 1990: 209). Retzinger and Scheff (1996) have also pointed out how restorative justice works as a powerful ritual to repair broken social bonds (as have Braithwaite, 2000; Karstedt, 2006; and Maruna, 2011).

Maruna (2011) has noted how contemporary criminal justice processes fail at providing successful reintegration rituals. Our society has created elaborate spectacles of punishment, but nothing to reintroduce an offender back into society. He argued that such status-degradation ceremonies in criminal justice, without adequate status-elevation ceremonies on the other end, have negative consequences and that status-elevating 'redemptive rituals' are needed to symbolize to an offender that he is part of a moral community. Restorative justice programmes are examples of such a ritual. Indeed, Braithwaite and Mugford (1994) specified the conditions under which a restorative justice encounter can be a successful reintegration ritual as including the decoupling of the offence from the perpetrator, by ensuring the presence of supporters, empowering victims, and encouraging respectful interactions.

Short-Term Outcomes

A successful interaction ritual has long-term and short-term outcomes. Short-term outcomes include positive feelings of group solidarity and a momentary rise in emotional energy. This solidarity creates symbols of group membership which remind participants of these positive feelings and, theoretically, extend the high emotional energy to future interaction rituals.

Solidarity, shared morality, and short-term emotional energy

A successful interaction ritual is marked by a number of ritual outcomes, including displays of solidarity, a sense of shared morality, and a feeling of emotional energy. Solidarity is externalized when people synchronize their body movements and take part in conversational turn-taking (Collins, 2004: 66). In high solidarity interactions conversation will flow more easily, there will be fewer embarrassing silences (see Goffman, 1956), and people will make eye contact and touch each other more often than in lower solidarity interactions. This contributes to a general feeling of group membership marked by a shared morality in which participants are in agreement on what is right and good, and gain positive feelings from this mutual agreement.

In a restorative justice conference one can observe a rise in solidarity between the offender, victim, and supporters as the conference progresses. This may be externalized by a lessening of gaps in conversation, increased eye contact between participants, a synchronization of sounds such as group crying or laughing, and touching—hugs, handshakes, or pats on the shoulder.

Solidarity in a successful interaction ritual is accompanied by a momentary burst of emotional energy or 'buzz' that arises from the social interaction. In fact, Collins uses restorative justice as an example of how an interaction can be turned into an emotional energy-creating ritual (Collins, 2004: 111). While this emotional energy can be seen and measured during an interaction ritual, it is most powerful as a long-term emotion—this will be discussed further in Chapter Seven. In a restorative justice conference, these externalizations of emotional energy can be observed in the body posture and facial expressions of individuals. For example, offenders who sit hunched over, downcast, and disengaged at the beginning of the conference may be sitting upright and smiling by the end. Emotional energy states can also be evaluated through interviews about a person's emotions and attitudes.

Symbolic representation

A successful interaction ritual creates strong collective symbols that act as a reminder of group membership and solidarity. These tide individuals over between interaction rituals. Without them, the consequences of the interaction may just be fleeting.

Can restorative justice conferences provide meaningful symbols? A useful way of thinking about this is by making the distinction offered by Retzinger and Scheff (1996) between material and symbolic reparation. Material reparations include an undertaking agreed upon by participants that repairs the harm—often through compensation, restitution, or community service. This negotiation happens towards the end of a conference, when participants conventionally formulate and sign an outcome agreement or a plan for action. This agreement may note if an apology was made and accepted but primarily lists instrumental steps the offender agrees to take. Copies are made for each participant to take home with them. These agreements, while focusing on material reparation, can potentially serve as a symbol of the interaction that has taken place, although, in reality, they often feel 'tacked on' to the end of the conference, well after the emotional peak or displays of solidarity.

In Retzinger and Scheff's conception, symbolic reparation is the real heart of the conference and 'it is the vital element that differentiates conferences from all other forms of crime control' (Retzinger and Scheff, 1996: 317). The core sequence of symbolic reparation involves an expression of shame or remorse by the offender, and some sign or gesture of forgiveness by the victim (or at least the hint that forgiveness may be possible somewhere down the line). This type of reparation is more effective at repairing broken bonds between offender and victim, and also comes to symbolize the potential for repairing bonds broken between an offender and their family, support system, and larger community. Retzinger and Scheff argued that material reparation is not likely to be considered effective, or meaningful, without symbolic reparation. Similarly, in Bennett (2008) the symbolic meaning of an 'apology ritual' in criminal justice is the foundation of his theory of punishment. He argued that we want to make an offender 'act as she would were she genuinely sorry for her offence' (Bennett, 2008: 146). Perhaps this exchange of remorse and forgiveness between offender and victim, even if only fleeting and lasting a few seconds, can act as a powerful symbol of the social bond.

This may be problematic, however, when apology is virtually built into the script. Once the participants have expressed how they have been affected by the crime, the facilitator will often turn to the offender and ask if there is anything they would like to say and they are practically compelled to offer an apology at this point. While there are many instances of spontaneous apology and expressions of forgiveness in conferences, relying on a formal apology at this point may not create an effective apology ritual, or be filled with the symbolic meaning described by Retzinger and Scheff. While the strength of these symbols is an empirical issue that can be measured, perhaps the memory of the emotional peak in the interaction is sufficient to ensure short- and long-term benefits.

Long-Term Outcomes

In interaction rituals the group symbols and feelings of solidarity created lead to a short-term, transient emotion or buzz. Such instances of solidarity and emotional energy also have the potential to be translated into a long-term emotional state that, theoretically, the participants can add to their stock of symbols and emotional energy and take into future solidarity-creating interactions as part of an 'interaction ritual chain' (Collins, 2004).

Having experienced the emotional energy from a successful interaction ritual, individuals will need to participate in other interaction rituals in order to maintain, or increase, their emotional energy. This is because emotional energy decays over time and the benefits of the initial interaction decrease. So, like a battery, the individual will need to engage in more solidarity-producing interactions in order to be 'recharged'. Once the initial interaction ritual ends, the individual enters a kind of interactional market (Collins, 1993) where they will endeavour to reinvest their current stocks of emotional energy in future interaction rituals. The more they invest, the bigger the long-term payoff. In this process, people become emotional energy seekers, always moving towards the highest emotional energy payoffs they can find relative to their current resources.

A common criticism with shame and procedural justice theories of restorative justice is that they do not provide a realistic account of the long-term effects of a conference. The restorative justice conference is usually a single intervention. What good could one instance of reintegrative or acknowledged shame do in the life of an offender? How could it affect someone whose life may be characterized by stigmatizing interactions and where shame, anger, and violence are a part of everyday life? As with most theory and research on emotion in which the focus is on short-term or transient emotions, little attention has been paid to long-term emotional states (Collins, 1990). Long-term emotional energy, however, may theoretically be the most important issue in setting out a social theory of human behaviour. In restorative justice, long-term emotional energy may prove to be the key that keeps people from reoffending.

For an offender with a low stock of emotional energy prior to a restorative justice conference—especially if they are a repeat offender who has already experienced rituals of stigmatic shame in the courts, prisons, or probation and parole—they may desire emotional energy but lack the necessary resources to invest in positive interaction rituals. Alternatively, they may invest in an interaction ritual that provides some emotional energy, such as the rush incurred by committing a crime (Katz, 1988), but this will soon end when they are compelled to participate in a series of status-reducing interactions such as attending court or receiving a prison sentence.

Emotional energy does not have to be created from previous stocks of emotional energy, it can also be created 'out of thin air' by a particularly intense interaction ritual. According to Collins, interaction ritual is a mechanism of change: 'as long as there are potential occasions for ritual mobilization, there is the possibility for sudden and abrupt periods of change' (Collins, 2004: 43). In the case of restorative justice, a powerful interaction may tip the emotional energy scales in the offender's favour, and encourage them to seek out interactions that will top up their emotional energy.

While an actual restorative justice conference may not be repeated, the emotional energy gained from the single interaction may be the key to motivating a person to engage in further positive interactions that lead to a reduction in offending. Seen from this perspective, it is not reintegrative shame, acknowledged shame, or any other particular emotion at work that makes restorative justice successful. Instead, it may be that a taste of emotional energy leaves an individual hungry for more positive interactions, thus motivating them to engage in pro-social behaviour.

Power and Status Rituals

Power and status are further aspects of interaction rituals that influence each other and lead to stratified rituals. Broadly speaking, power rituals in an interaction determine who is an 'order giver' and who is an 'order taker' while status rituals show the extent to which an individual is part of a group. People who have power and status in an interaction are more likely to have more positive long-term benefits in the form of emotional energy.

In the restorative justice conference, power dynamics may influence the outcome so the aim in an ideal conference will be to try to circumvent this. As all participants are supposed to be on an equal footing—engaging in democratic deliberation—a conference that is stratified along power dimensions is likely to fail. Similarly, in conferences where people take on the roles of order-giver and order-taker the interaction may be dominated by one participant (either offender or victim). In such cases, there will be low emotional energy (or perhaps unacknowledged, or stigmatizing, shame) on the part of the order-taker.

During a conference there is always the potential for the status of the offender to change. Initially, the victims, as the wronged party, are most likely to have the moral upper hand. By the end of a conference, however, the offender's status may be elevated as they come to be accepted by the victim and their supporters as a member of the social group. The victim's acceptance of the offender as a 'good' person will raise their status and, consequently, the emotional energy. In an unsuccessful conference, the victim will not accept the offender as a person on the same level as them, further depleting emotional energy.

To summarize, when examining restorative justice conferences as interaction rituals one must do so with an eye to the potential status and power imbalances. If we reconceptualize restorative justice conferences as a form of interaction ritual we can theorize how the process serves both restorative and deterrence functions. Through rhythmic coordination and the emotional entrainment that happens over time during the course of conversation, participants will become charged up with feelings of solidarity, group membership, and emotional energy by the conclusion of a conference. Ideally this will create some kind of collective symbol and positive feelings that will follow individuals into future interactions, helping them to engage in further emotional energy-building rituals.

For offenders, this kind of interaction may provide them with just enough emotional energy to motivate them to stop (or at least reduce) offending. All of these propositions can be empirically tested and in Chapters Four to Seven of this book I will analyse elements of this theory through a combination of qualitative and quantitative methods.

Are Good Rituals Driving the Success of Restorative Justice?

While shame and procedural justice theories do a good job of identifying specific emotions at work in restorative justice, they do not specify how emotions and behaviour can be transformed through such a process. Ritual theories, specifically Collins's theory of interaction ritual chains (Collins, 2004), can fill this gap. The reason 'emotional' conferences are 'good' conferences is that the emotions are used to create a strong interaction ritual which results in feelings of solidarity and emotional energy. This is generally felt by all present, as seen when the facilitator returns from 'good' conferences on a high, eager to share the experiences with colleagues. As Chapter Five will show, facilitators employ a number of strategies to create the necessary ingredients for a successful interaction ritual and emotions truly are at the heart of their success. Expressions of strong emotions in the conference (be it anger, fear, or shame) often act as a turning point that allows the participants to develop a shared rhythm to their interaction. Facilitators are trained to be attuned to these as the careful way emotions are incited and expressed allows for a shared mood, rhythm, and balance of power that results in expressions of solidarity and shared morality.

A number of questions arise from this discussion of emotions and ritual. What does an interaction ritual actually look like? How can we observe and analyse one? Can we develop an empirical model for interaction ritual in restorative justice that tests the conditions under which a restorative justice conference can lead to solidarity, feelings of group membership, and a symbolic representation of these emotions? Can this model predict the likelihood of future offending? In Chapter Four I explore the ritual dynamics of a single conference in-depth and in Chapter Five examine how facilitators prepare for a successful conference and use strategies to ensure that the ingredients are present for a successful ritual. I discuss what short-term outcomes, like solidarity, actually look and feel like and then present a statistical model of interaction ritual in restorative justice using quantitative data collected by systematic observations of conferences in Chapter Six. Finally, in Chapter Seven I will examine how successful interaction rituals are related to offending behaviour after a conference.

Methodological Approaches to Studying Ritual

The research uses a three-pronged approach to studying the micro dynamics of restorative justice conferences. This involves a combination of qualitative interviews; detailed observations of discourse, face and demeanour; and the quantitative analysis of systematically observed conferences. I focus on displays of emotions, emotional turning points, and the emergence of rhythm and solidarity between participants as the key to successful short-and long-term outcomes, demonstrating the impact of emotionally successful conferences on recidivism.

Qualitative data

The qualitative data consists of in-depth interviews with police facilitators. These facilitators were employed to work at the Justice Research Consortium, which was conducting a trial of restorative justice for serious adult offenders being prosecuted for robbery or burglary in the Crown Courts of London (see Shapland et al, 2004). Upon entering a guilty plea, but before sentencing, the experimental group of offenders took part in a police-led, face-to-face restorative justice conference with their victim, which was also attended by supporters on both sides—usually close relatives or friends.

The control group received no treatment outside ordinary prosecu-tion. Due to the serious nature of the offences, most offenders were on remand in custody awaiting sentence. This meant that approxi-mately eighty-five per cent of the conferences were held in prison and the rest were held in police stations and community centres. Conferences lasted about two hours, at which point an outcome agreement was drafted by the facilitator, signed by all those present, and submitted before the judge, who had the discretion to take it into account while sentencing.

In order to gain a deeper understanding of how facilitators distinguish between conferences, I conducted in-depth interviews with facilitators about conferences they chose to be their 'best', 'worst', and 'typical' conferences. Together, we mapped out all of the events leading up to, and during, the conference, examining each situation in detail. All facilitators categorized their best con-ferences as being the most emotionally intense, and their worst as either emotionally flat or very intense for one party but not the other. The interview guide used to explore these conferences can be found in Appendix 1.

Eight police officers served as facilitators on the research team, with most facilitators having significant experience of running twelve or more conferences. I interviewed each of them on three separate occasions about their most successful, typical, and least successful cases, which resulted in a total of twenty-four situational analyses. This sample size is directly proportionate to the number of facilitators on the original research team, all of whom I inter-viewed. I systematically coded the interviews based on components of interaction ritual as described by Collins (2004), such as rhythm, emotional entrainment, and solidarity. Additionally, I reviewed all the case logs and observer reports of these conferences. This analysis maps out the dynamics of a successful restorative justice conference by comparing solidarity-creating interactions with less successful rituals. By making these comparisons, I aim to identify the micro level elements of such rituals to build a theory of how emotions and interactions work in restorative justice.

There are two ways of thinking about how to study emotions. One is based on the idea that emotions are an interior experience and a careful interviewer can bring them to the surface. The other way considers emotions to be an external thing, a Durkheimian social fact that can be observed and documented. This is the per-spective utilized by contemporary sociologists of emotion such as

Jack Katz, Thomas Scheff and Suzanne Retzinger, who base their analysis not on direct interviews with participants, but on detailed examination of what people do in an interaction.

Facilitator accounts are the ideal source of data when examining the elements of interaction ritual. Although interviews with conference participants can shed light on their subjective experience of the conference, in the style of Goffman, I am committed to the study of encounters, with the group as the unit of analysis rather than the individual. To prioritize the group-focus with this data, it is appropriate to rely on the facilitators' accounts of each case, as they are the ones who are trained to be attuned to group-level dynamics. Indeed, as Collins suggests (2004: 97), when studying interaction rituals one should begin with powerful symbols—in this case conferences that especially resonated with facilitators—and work backwards from there. Once we have identified an interaction that strikes us as particularly emblematic, we then,

Reconstruct as best as possible what IRs have surrounded that emblem. Who assembled, in what numbers, with what frequency or schedule? What emotions were expressed, what activities brought a focus of attention, what intensity of collective effervescence was generated? To what degree were individual participants charged with emotional energy; and what did it motivate them to do? What were the barriers to participation; who was divided by the ritual from whom? Who was thereby ranked over whom? (Collins, 2004: 97)

In the context of restorative justice conferences, the facilitator is ideally placed to reveal such elements. Their role requires them to keep track of who made eye contact with whom, who leaned forward to engage, who pulled away to disengage, who was disruptive, and who caused an imbalance. Such dynamics are keenly documented by the facilitator, who must respond to them in the process of guiding the conference along.

Facilitators also have the unique perspective of not being directly involved in the proceedings and can therefore provide accounts of what is happening at the group level. Conference participants may not be very good observers of what happens in an interaction; they are more focused on their own experience and making sense of what it all means, and so may not be attuned to the micro details of emotional expression, body posturing, and tone of others, and how these lead to turning points and a shared rhythm. Facilitators are not infallible, and the accounts they provide can never be fully objective (nor could those of an external observer); however, they have the experience and training to report on the micro level dynamics of how the conference unfolds in space and time.

In addition to the interviews with all facilitators on the original research team, I reviewed all the police case logs and observer summaries of these particular conferences. As a member of the research team for two years, I participated in facilitator training with the Metropolitan Police; accompanied the facilitators on home visits as they met with victims and offenders; observed many of their conferences; and liaised with the many criminal justice agencies involved in getting this project off the ground. While my own impressions helped to shape the study, the data I present here are based on facilitators' recollections of conferences and the detailed notes of the conference written up in narrative form by an observer from the Consortium's research team.

By examining solidarity-creating situations in-depth, and comparing them to less successful interactions, one can begin to map the dynamics of a restorative justice conference. The amount of detail the facilitators recalled was remarkable and the strongest message I took away from my time with them was that organizing a conference is extremely difficult and time-consuming. It requires emotional sensitivity and the ability to strategize and problem solve. These facilitators put great effort into each conference and felt elated when it was a 'success' and very let down when it 'failed'. Because they were so professionally and emotionally invested in the process, they remembered fine details about their conferences long after the event.

To supplement these situational analyses of conferences, I also interviewed six offenders who participated in a restorative justice conference. They are not a representative sample of all restorative justice offenders but were nominated by facilitators based on the criteria that their offences were more serious than most, and they were all sentenced to prison for at least six months. I met with these men between eighteen months and two years after their conference took place. Some had completed their prison sentence and had been released, some were still serving their sentence, and one had served his sentence but was back in prison on another offence. Ten offenders were nominated and I was able to interview six. Influenced by the life course perspective developed by Maruna (2001) and Laub and Sampson (2003), I explore how they talk about their conference long after it took place, and how they do or do not use it to shape a life course narrative. With a larger sample size, this could have been a major study on its own. As it stands, the interviews provide useful insight into how *some* offenders interpret the role restorative justice played in their lives, and connects micro sociological theory to life course studies. This small sample cannot be used to generalize about the long-term impact of restorative justice, but can provide some insight into how offenders talk about their experience of it. These interviews also help evaluate the long-term effects of inter-action ritual. As I will discuss, the ritual outcome of emotional energy is a long-term, ongoing process. People are filled with high or low levels of emotional energy based on their ongoing interac-tional contexts. The best way to assess this is by following par-ticipants over time to examine how any emotional energy created in a conference is transmitted through future interactions. In my interviews I attempt to trace their emotional energy states since their conference.

A final source of qualitative data was a video recording of a restorative justice conference held for a robbery in London. This case was originally in the Justice Research Consortium experiment with the Metropolitan Police, but was taken out of the study so that it could be filmed for training and educational purposes. It consisted of a conference between a victim, offender, and their supporters and was facilitated by one of the Justice Research Consortium police facilitators. It is a good example of the types of conferences run by the Metropolitan Police, and I use it to conduct a fine-grained analysis of the ritual elements of such a conference.

Quantitative data

The qualitative data provide an in-depth and thick description of the restorative justice process. This can be supplemented by a quantitative analysis of the ritual elements. Can we statistically model the structure of a restorative justice interaction ritual? Can we use this model to examine whether these ritual elements are related to reoffending? This is one more piece of the puzzle, linking together micro and mezzo elements.

The data to explore and test this theory are drawn from the Reintegrative Shaming Experiments ('RISE'), a restorative justice experiment conducted in Canberra, Australia, between 1995 and 2000. Upon arrest for an eligible offence, and admission of guilt at the police station, offenders were immediately asked to participate in the trial. If they consented, they were randomly assigned into one of two groups: the control group (where they were prosecuted as normal) and an experimental group of people diverted from prosecution into a restorative justice conference. The restorative justice conference consisted of a police-led, face-to-face meeting between the offender and the victim, as well as a number of supporters from both the offender's and victim's side.[1]

This study focuses on two of the four experiments conducted in Canberra: juvenile violence and juvenile personal property.[2] The Juvenile Violent Crime experiment involved violent offences (assaults and robberies) committed by people below 30 years old (although in practice most were under eighteen). The Juvenile Personal Property experiment consisted of property crimes that involved a personal victim. Offences in this experiment included burglaries, thefts, and criminal damage. A member of the research team observed each conference, and then completed a survey documenting their systematic observations. The experiment was developed in response to Braithwaite's original 1989 theory (hence the name), so many of the observations focused on measuring reintegrative or stigmatizing shaming, or shame behaviour. Many of the items, however, are also particularly relevant to developing measures for ritual variables. This will be further discussed in Chapter Six.

The RISE experiment is widely known in the restorative justice community. The various datasets have been subject many times to analysis and re-analysis and continue to reveal new insights into restorative justice.[3] In many ways it has set the standard for how restorative justice is researched and evaluated. Portions of the data have been used to compare conferencing versus court in terms of reoffending (Sherman, Strang, and Woods, 2000); victim perspectives

---

[1] For a detailed description of eligibility criteria and experimental design, see Sherman et al (1998).

[2] The other two experiments consisted of adults arrested after failing random alcohol tests at road checkpoints, and juveniles arrested for shoplifting at corporate stores where their offence was detected by store personnel. The offence criteria of these conferences precluded a face-to-face meeting with a personal victim. In order to keep the structures of the conferences consistent for the purposes of this study, only experiments that involved direct contact between offender and victim were included. However, future research may examine interactional dynamics in conferences when there was no victim present.

[3] The data include the systematic observations of conferences and court, multiple waves of surveys of both offenders and victims, and official police records from the Australian Federal Police.

(Strang, 2002); procedural justice (Barnes, 1999; Tyler et al, 2007), and shame and shaming (Harris, 2001, 2003). I have tried to do something new with this landmark data. While these experiments were designed as randomized controlled trials (the gold standard of policy evaluation), data from the control groups is not utilized in this analysis. In the RISE experiment, the conference cases were diverted entirely from prosecution and the control cases were prosecuted as normal. This usually involved a brief hearing before the judge (often less than ten minutes), where the young offenders usually pleaded guilty while their lawyers negotiated a sentence for them. While fascinating interaction rituals in their own right, these court appearances are qualitatively different from a two hour face-to-face meeting between offender and victim. Court-conference comparisons are useful when testing the effectiveness of restorative justice as a policy; however, as Braithwaite (2002) suggestsed they are not helpful in developing a theory of restorative justice. Rather, I agree with Hayes and Daly (2003) that it is through the study of variations within conferences that an understanding of how they work can develop. Therefore, my analysis focuses on the explicit micro interactions of participants, grounded in interaction ritual theory, and uses the conference data to make this a true test of the variations within restorative justice conferences.[4]

Using Mixed Methods to Build Theory

Influenced by micro sociologists such as Collins (2004, 2008), Scheff (1990), and Katz (2001) I have been purposely eclectic in my data collection, drawing from a range of sources and conditions. Taken together, this is a multifaceted approach to examining interaction rituals in restorative justice that encompasses an exploration of how rituals unfold dynamically in space and time (Chapter Four); situational analyses of successful and failed rituals (Chapters Five and Six); an empirical test of interaction ritual theory in restorative justice using systematic observations of conferences (Chapter Six); and an investigation of the long-term effects of such rituals, both

[4] In addition to these theoretical arguments, I conducted a preliminary analysis of the data that included both conferences and court cases. I found that having a conference was the largest predictor of whether the interaction ritual was a success. This suggests that there are distinct differences between conference and court, and it may not be useful to compare them as interaction rituals when developing a theory of restorative justice.

through quantitative modelling of how ritual can impact offending and how offenders talk about the role restorative justice played in their lives (Chapter Seven). These methods, levels of analysis, and theoretical approaches are combined to develop a micro theory of restorative justice.

I kept this multifaceted approach in mind as I conducted my fieldwork and when I was developing my analytic procedures. The themes that I uncovered through my interviews acted as signposts—orientating me and providing focus when I conducted the analysis of the video. They also helped to develop and interpret the statistical constructs and their relationship to each other. In this way, the different types of data speak to each other, providing a full and round account of how emotions and rituals work in restorative justice conferences. Certainly there will be flaws, but this study is the first of its kind to systematically explore and statistically model micro level variations in the restorative justice process.

4

A Micro Analysis of Restorative Justice[1]

Restorative justice is generally evaluated retrospectively, using survey data about restoration to individual victims or the community, participant satisfaction, or by measuring reoffending. While this valuable research has extended the range of stakeholders considered in responding to crime to include victims and communities (Robinson and Shapland, 2008), scholars have begun calling for closer inspection and documentation of the dynamics of the conference process (Braithwaite, 2002, 2006; Daly, 2001; Daly and Stubbs, 2006; Harris, Walgrave, and Braithwaite, 2004).

This chapter considers the restorative justice encounter itself, and presents an analysis of how the process works at the micro level to organize emotions, facilitate interactions, and build relationships. Developing Collins's theory of interaction ritual chains (Collins, 2004), I provide a detailed reading of a single conference to map the emotional and interactional dynamics, working in this case to transform a situation of anger and anxiety into one marked by displays of solidarity between victim, offender, and family. In doing so, I develop a methodological framework for a more rigorous analysis of the dynamics of the restorative justice processes.

Case Study Approach

The in-depth analysis of a single event is a theoretically useful, and empirically rigorous, exercise (Arendt, 1963; Maynard and Manzo, 1993; Scheff, 1990; Shaw, 1966) that allows us to document the development of emotions and interaction ritual concepts

[1] A version of this chapter was published earlier in M. Rossner, 'Emotions and Interaction Ritual: A Micro Analysis of Restorative Justice' (2011) 51(1) *British Journal of Criminology* 95.

over time. Collins has suggested that direct observation is the best way to examine the dynamics of an interaction ritual (Collins, 2004: 134) and the following analysis is based on direct observation of a videotaped restorative justice conference. The benefit of using the videotape is that it allows us to slow down, pause, and rewind in order to document the real-time development of the conference.

One may ask whether an analysis of one case can help us develop a theory of restorative justice. Indeed, it would be foolish to develop a full theory based on a single case. However, combined with other approaches, the case study presented in this chapter provides a meaningful investigation into the micro dynamics of emotion and ritual in restorative justice. My case study analysis of the micro dynamics is inspired by an ethnomethodological and interactionist perspective on ritual (for example, as found in Scheff's analysis of discourses and emotion in passages of Goethe's *The Sorrows of Young Werther* and Eliot's *Middlemarch* (Scheff, 1990); Goffman's study of confidence men, mental patients, or upper class pleasantries (Goffman, 1959, 1967); Katz's study of a police interrogation (Katz, 1999); or Garfinkel's study of becoming transgendered (Garfinkel, 1967). In different ways, these examples all use case studies to closely analyse the dynamics of interaction in order to develop a theory and the number of cases is less important than the revealing insights they can offer about human interaction and the social order.

Another analogy to this is Manyard and Manzo's paper on justice and dynamics in a jury deliberation (Manyard and Manzo, 1993). Using one video recording of a criminal jury deliberation, they elegantly explored how jurors talk about justice and the games they play to reach a desired outcome. They did not propose to generalize about how jurors deliberate based on this close-reading, but instead provided an insightful look at the micro dynamics of the jury room. Following such examples, this chapter explores what is happening inside the circle at a restorative justice conference.

In the video, we see what emotions the offender, victim, and supporters convey at the start of the conference. We see how emotions are expressed as the conference progresses, and how a conversational and bodily rhythm emerges from the initial disjointed and awkward conversation. Finally, the video illustrates how solidarity can arise out of the conflict between victim and offender.

Methodologies

This chapter relies on two theoretical and analytic strategies to examine interaction ritual and emotion in restorative justice. The first perspective draws from research by Ekman and colleagues who, over the last forty years, have developed a facial coding scheme identifying the key micro movements and expressions in a person's face that reveal emotion (Ekman and Friesen, 1975; Ekman and Rosenberg, 1998). While any attempt to 'read' emotions is rightfully met with some resistance (see Turner, 2000, for a summary of the debate), over many years of looking at faces of all ages, sexes, cultural, ethnic, and racial backgrounds, Ekman identified the universal facial movements associated with happiness, sadness, anger, fear, surprise, and disgust and has shown how these facial movements can be combined, masked, and emphasized to express different emotions. My analysis employs a modified version of Ekman's facial coding scheme to examine participants' emotions during the conference—these include anxiety, fear, anger, and disgust (Ekman and Friesen, 1975)—and presents stills from the conference videotape to discuss the way these emotions change as the conference progresses.

Secondly, excerpts of monologues and exchanges are presented using a modified conversation analysis of discourse, linguistic, and paralinguistic cues. This allows examination of turn-taking and other conversational 'rules' (Sacks, Schegloff, and Jefferson, 1974). Transcription conventions are adapted from Jefferson's widely used notations (Atkinson and Heritage, 1984). Non-verbal cues such as nodding, hand gestures, and posture are also coded and used in this analysis. These cues, along with actual dialogue, reveal the structure of the interaction ritual.

This analysis relies on metaphors of dramaturgy and game playing in interaction (Goffman, 1967, 1981). Goffman pointed out the many games we play in conversation as we vie for power and status. He introduced many valuable concepts that help us understand the micro dynamics of an interaction ritual such as footing, face, accounts, and impression management. Influenced by this perspective, Scheff (1990) has been a pioneer in examining emotions and interactions. He drew on a wide variety of sources (including recordings of family members interacting and excerpts from works of fiction) to explore the micro dynamics of emotions such as shame and embarrassment. The visual analysis pioneered by Ekman allows us to specify and describe the dynamic patterns of emotions as they happen in an interaction ritual, taking the perspective developed by Goffman, Scheff, and Collins one step further.

In conducting this analysis through a video recording, I had the luxury not available through live observation of pausing, slowing down, and rewinding the interaction. A drawback of using film is that when viewing events through a camera lens, you are presented with an interpretation based on what images the filmmaker and editor decide to focus on. It is fortunate in this case that while one cannot see all the faces all the time, the audio has not been edited, and the film captures the dynamic way emotions are displayed, rhythm is developed, participants become mutually focused, and solidarity is externalized. This is a rare and valuable source of data as such conferences are rarely videotaped.

The bulk of the analysis in this chapter relies on direct observation of the film, focusing on what the participants say to each other and how they say it. Consistent with an approach used by micro sociologists studying a range of social interactions, this is a useful way to examine the dynamics of an interaction ritual. Interviews with participants could also provide a valuable source of data on how they interpret their emotional states during, and after, the conference. Consequently, in this case, brief exit interviews were conducted by the film crew with each participant. Their responses can help interpret the emotional dynamics of the conference and confirm, or disconfirm, what was observed.

In the next section, I describe the robbery based on a reconstruction of events described by conference participants. I then explore the emotions and tensions in the room as the conference begins. I examine key moments of dialogue and monologue, highlighting instances where the conference develops a rhythm and emotional climaxes act as turning points. I also show how the balance of the interaction can be offset, and how participants may be emotionally manipulated. Finally, I explore how positive outcomes, such as solidarity, are displayed at the end of the conference. I conclude by offering an evaluation of the success of the conference as an interaction ritual.

A London Mugging

On a sunny afternoon, Anne is walking through the park in her London neighbourhood chatting with her daughter on her mobile phone. They are making plans to meet in a few moments at a nearby café. Anne hangs up the phone and places it in her handbag, which is slung over her shoulder.

As she continues through the park, she feels a tug at her shoulder. Thinking it is her daughter, she turns around to see Aaron pulling up the hood of his sweatshirt to cover his face. He grabs the bag and tries to run away, but she holds onto the long strap and the ensuing struggle ends only when Aaron violently jerks the bag out of her hands, twisting her fingers in the process. He starts to run through the park, with Anne chasing after him, and is about to duck into an alleyway when he collides with a patrolling police officer who knocks him down and detains him. As soon as he hits the ground, Aaron starts sobbing, exclaiming, 'I'm sorry, I'm sorry! I didn't mean to do it!'

Aaron is taken into custody and spends the next few hours being processed and charged, eventually released on bail. He appears in court a few days later, pleading guilty to robbery. The judge warns him that recent sentences for this type of crime have resulted in significant prison time—a response intended to curb a rising epidemic of mobile phone thefts.

After his hearing, Aaron and his wife Gillian are approached by Mark, a Metropolitan Police officer, who offers them a chance to meet with Anne and her husband, Terry. They all agree to meet and be videotaped for training purposes. The conference takes place in a disused police station a few days prior to Aaron's sentence.

Conference Beginnings: Emotional Build-Up

As the conference begins, it is striking to see the differences in the demeanour, dress, and facial expressions of the participants. Aaron walks into the room first. Tall and skinny, he appears to be in his mid-twenties and his accent reveals a working class, Irish background. He wears a plaid button down shirt, the top few buttons undone to reveal tattoos on his chest, creeping up and around his neck towards his shaved head. The backs of his hands and wrists are also tattooed. His face is pockmarked and scarred. His eyebrow is pierced with a silver bar, his ears with gold hoops and studs. Around his neck is a thick gold chain.

As he walks to his seat, he is frowning slightly and his mouth is pursed. His eyebrows and forehead are tense, with deep wrinkles on his brow and in between his eyes. Once seated, he clasps his hands in front of him, periodically wringing them and fidgeting nervously. His chin is tucked, so he appears to look up when he speaks. He continually looks to Mark for reassurance and speaks in terse, short sentences. He pauses, often mid-sentence, and a fleeting expression of panic/fear comes over his face. In these moments, his eyes widen and his lower face becomes slack. His brow remains raised and drawn together, but the lower parts of his eyes become tense. This could be an example of facial deceit—micro expressions lasting less than half a second which indicate someone trying to hide their true emotion. Aaron's micro expressions may reveal concealed fear (Ekman, 2001).

Unlike her husband, whose distinctive look stands out in a crowd, Gillian blends in. Her brown hair is pulled back and reveals a clear face with wide eyes. She wears jeans underneath a long coat. She speaks articulately, and has a general look and demeanour that suggests she is more adept at 'passing' in different social circles than her partner. Her social skills allow her to act as a bridge between Aaron and the middle class Anne and Terry, and she will play a pivotal role in the conference. Throughout the conference, Gillian holds their eighteen-month-old son, who sucks on a dummy and drifts in and out of sleep. While Aaron's face shows a combination of fear and anxiety, Gillian looks inquisitive. Her large eyes stare intently at whomever is talking, biting her lower lip in concentration. She appears attentive, nodding and murmuring in agreement when others speak.

Anne and her husband, Terry, are white, middle class professionals. She is a journalist at a major national newspaper and he is a headmaster at a local school. Like many Londoners, they live in a pleasant neighbourhood that borders a poorer, and more dangerous, one. They have four grown children, all of whom are either at university or working.

Anne and Terry are already seated when Aaron, Gillian, and the baby enter the room. The camera focuses on Anne's face as she watches Aaron cross the room to his seat. Her greying brown hair is styled in a simple, short cut and she is dressed casually in jeans and a jumper. As she watches Aaron, a range of emotions are apparent on her face. Her eyes slope downwards, as do the corners of her mouth. At the same time, her eyes are slightly widened and drawn together, suggesting fear. She turns her lips up to smile in greeting a number of times, but each instance lasts a fraction of a second, immediately turning back into a frown. She smiles with only the lower half of her face, not activating her middle or upper brow. This is similar to what psychologists call a 'Pan-American' smile, after the pasted on facial expressions of flight attendants (Seligman, 2002). This superficial movement of the mouth suggests an attempt at facial deceit, or a masking of her true emotion (Ekman, 2001).

Her husband, Terry, on the other hand, does not mask his feelings. He is heavyset and ruddy, with a thick neck, close cropped greying

Figure 4.1 Pan-Am Smile

hair, a beard, and close-set eyes. As Aaron and Gillian walk into the room, the anger on his face is visible. His eyes narrow to slits as he stares straight ahead. His lips are pursed and the tension around his mouth is evident. In one instance, his hand is clenched in a fist that he holds to his chin. Periodically, he rubs his hands on his thighs, almost readying himself to pounce. His whole body is taut, resembling a coiled spring.

The participants' facial expressions illustrate a variety of emotions at the start of the conference: a mix of fear and anxiety on the faces of Anne and Aaron; anger on Terry's; and anxiety and concentration on Gillian's. While we do not know at this point how the conference will progress, there is the potential for emotional intensity.

Figure 4.2 Anger

Developing a Rhythm

The conference begins with Mark asking Aaron to recount in detail how the robbery took place. The following excerpt is from the first two minutes of the conference. Words and sounds are phonetically replicated, while still following standard spelling conventions. Consistent with conversational analytic methods, my notations also indicate short pauses (demarcated by an ellipsis), longer pauses (the number of seconds in parentheses), and drawn out sounds (demarcated by colons and repeated letters). Full stops and commas are used for natural pauses and sentence conclusions. Letters and words in brackets represent overlapping speech. I also include in double parentheses significant non-verbal cues, such as nodding and head shaking.

[1:36]

1 **Aaron**: Usshhhun, I'd just like to tank, wuh, thank you for agreein tuh… come

2 and seeuh, agreein tuh come and sat I'm bad with my words. And. I'd

3 just like to thank you…. very much…for comin…an::d your husband.

4 n::::: I'm very sorry for wha::ha for what I did. I ain' that…I ain't that

5 type of person…to go out and do that. It's the first time I ev… ever

6	done anything like that. (1) m:: basically what happened was:: m:: hada
7	mm hada bad week. Pt pt basically I had pth been outta work for a
8	coupla months. h::: I've my kneecap broken h::. (1) huh Gon the social
9	wannt payin us properly. Weh, havin a bad, no one to help us. No family.
10	In this country. My…only had my dad uh in this country but I don't get
11	on with? H::: sh::: jus::t basically we have no food (1) we had no electric
12	no gas…in in our flat. Nnd we're ar::guing…me and Gillian, theah the
13	a day of the incident. Me and Gillian were arguing all that morning.. .
14	cus the baby had been screamin sh::: been hungry. We were hungry. (1)
15	ituh just got a bit too much. Everybody was…all my friends, I was
16	asking for for un a coupla pounds they just couldn't afford to give it to
17	me they huuh handt any themselves. So I 'greed I just left left the flat
18	goin going to ask my dad even though I didn't get along with him. (1)
19	and I'm just on my way up. ohh walkin up the hill as as I was passing
20	yah. I don't know what got intuh (3.5) I just reached over uh and I took
21	your bag (1.5) and I ran. (2) n::: im really really sorry for it (2.5). If
22	there's anythin I can do (1) is…its to make, make up for it I'm willin to
23	duh it ((nodding head)). I know you probably don't…want, want me
24	anywheres near yuh. But they only way hyuh I know how to help people
25	is by doin something for em, like painting or::: mmyuh. I'm really good
26	with my hands and building. (6) ((Aaron and Anne both look at Mark))
27 Mark:	Aaron umm (1) take us through what happened when…you said you
28	ran. Take us through what happened when you ran. (2)

[3:42]

Aaron speaks for two minutes without any interruption. However, his speech is full of stutters and frequent pauses. He appears unsure of himself, apologizing for being 'bad with his words'. As the camera points to Anne, we see her nodding her head and focusing her eyes on Aaron. Although she is silent, her focused attention encourages him to continue his speech. Aaron's eyes dart back and forth, from quick looks up at Anne, then back down again, then over to Mark for reassurance.

During his monologue he relaxes and begins to settle into his speech. Around line eleven, the stutters and fillers begin to occur less frequently, and Aaron begins to talk in complete sentences. There are noticeable silences during particularly painful moments, such as when he describes taking the bag from Anne (3.5 seconds). There is also a 2.5 second pause at line twenty-one, when he finishes describing the robbery and apologizes. He seems to pause and wait for a response from Anne, but she is silent. To save face, Aaron continues to talk, moving away from talking about the robbery to offering to paint her house. This seems premature, and Anne and Terry do not respond.

The participants have been briefed by the facilitator about the three main components of a typical conference: a discussion of what happened; how everybody was harmed; and how to make things better. Aaron skips from part one to part three, and his offer is followed by an awkward six second pause. Both Aaron and Anne look helplessly towards Mark, with wide eyes and open mouths. He rescues the moment, bringing Aaron back to what happened, asking him to give more detail about his attempted escape.

At this point in the conference, Aaron is in the spotlight, forced to speak for long stretches of time without encouragement from the others. He stutters and pauses most when he has to explain his actions. He is more comfortable while talking about his family, or his background, or anything other than the actual robbery. The lack of input from the others adds to a disjointed feeling and lack of rhythm.

The scene changes once Anne begins to speak. She is reluctant at first, and Mark draws her out by asking a few leading questions. She focuses her eyes on Mark as she speaks, looking to him for encouragement. However, within a few seconds, her eyes move towards Aaron. While her facial expressions at the beginning of the conference suggest that she is anxious and afraid, her speech is markedly different from Aaron's.

[5:43]

1 **Anne:**   I mean, obviously, my questions, I take your apology, you did indeed

2   apologize at the time. Um and I recognize that you were genuinely

3   sorry…although I have to say very cynically I thought you were sorry

4   partly because you'd been caught at that stage. H::: um::::. (1.5) I mean I

5   I carry <u>every</u>thing in this purse. And this is the same purse. And I've also

6   got it always hooked the way it was at the time around my fingers. And,

7   as, what I was thinking as you ran was oh damn why didn't I notice him

8   coming because that is an area where people have been mug[ged be]fore

9 **Aaron:**   [Yeah] ((nods))

10 **Anne:**   And secondly, my passport's in there…that's my passport gone.. that is

11   <u>such</u> a nuisance, so it was kind of level of annoyance…. .

[6:08]

Anne speaks clearly and confidently, with less stuttering and fewer pauses. Aaron closely follows her, nodding in agreement at appropriate moments, such as when she remarks that the park is known for muggings. A few moments later she describes in greater detail the robbery from her perspective, and we see a rhythm begin to develop between them. In this dialogue, Aaron and Anne work together to develop the narrative.

[7:38]

1 **Anne:**   I saw you pull your hoodie up (1) and I 'sumed from that movement that

2   this was somebody who'd…was used to doing this sort of thing and you

3   were disguising your identity at that stage by pulling the hoodie straight

4   up.

5 **Aaron:**   ((nodding)) hhu:::gghh I ya I understand that yeah. When I was pullin

6   my hood up over ug[hs ((motions like he's pulling hood over his head))

7 **Anne:**   [Yeah

8 **Aaron:**   I have never I yah assure you I have never…. done anything like this

9   before. That why putting my face up so no one could

10   s[ee who I was]

11 **Anne:**   [mmm-uuhh][mm]

12 **Aaron:**   [cuz,] I dunno. I was confused at the time I dunno

13   what I was do[ing]

14 **Anne:**   [We]ll what I mean what what attracted you

15   about my bag what made you think that that

16 **Aaron:** I u::gh:: dunno, moment moment was goin through my head was just . . .

17   a quick bit of money. . .

18 **Anne:** Where does your father live?

19 **Aaron:** My father is situated…around Islington…..

[8:24]

In this section, Aaron and Anne respond positively to each other, even though they are discussing an uncomfortable topic. They are nodding, making eye contact, and sending cues that they are engaged. Their words very slightly overlap each other, a common component of high solidarity dialogue (Sacks, Schegloff, and Jefferson, 1974). She challenges Aaron's account of himself as 'not that type of person'. Although he maintains his line, he acknowledges that he understands her and respects her view. During this dialogue, they begin to develop a rhythm.

Anne and Aaron continue to have a series of exchanges in which he explains his background, his dysfunctional relationship with his abusive father, his family and money troubles, etc. Unlike his first attempt at speaking, where Anne regards him silently, she murmurs encouraging back channel signals: 'mmmm', etc (Macaulay, 2006). As he speaks, she looks at him interestedly with her head tilted slightly to the right, instead of straight on in an accusatory stare. She probes him, asking a number of follow-up questions about his family. Aaron's speech is much less disjointed as he clearly answers her questions about his family and background. He also empathizes with her, mentioning his own story of being the victim of a robbery, where he had his kneecaps broken.

While the above exchange is taking place between Aaron and Anne, the camera cuts to Terry. He is leaning back with his arms crossed across his large chest. He lets out a few audible sighs and looks around him. As he breathes, his chest rises and falls visibly, as if he is taking deep breaths to control himself. His eyes dart from Aaron to the room around him. He still has tension around his eyes, nose, and mouth. He moves his tongue around the inside of his cheek while Aaron is talking, pursing his lips. At times he rolls his eyes. While Anne and Aaron are slowly becoming rhythmically entrained with each other, Terry is not joining in on the flow. So far he has not spoken and does not appear involved in the interaction.

Figure 4.3 Lack of Engagement

After about thirty minutes, Mark asks Terry to explain how he has been affected. Terry describes the aftermath of the robbery, including the ongoing fear Anne and the rest of their family experience when walking through the park. Like Anne, Terry is sceptical of Aaron's story. However, he has not developed the same rapport as Aaron and Anne, and his accusations are not well received.

[29:08]

1	Terrry:	Ah:: and I've worked with a lot of people, as a teacher, who uhh'v been
2		in various sorts of trouble. Uh:: (deep breath) (1) And I must say, you

3		know, that you still <u>appear</u> to be somebody who is is in that market, if
4		you like. You know, the tattoos don't h[elp.]
5	Aaron:	[I kn]ow (1.5)
6	Terry:	To be perfectly frank with you. And your left hand looks as if it was
7		done in a very amateur sort of way. ((Aaron looks down at his
8		hands))And the people <u>I know</u> who've had that have usually been in
9		young offenders institutio[ns]
10	Aaron:	[Mm]m
11	Terry:	And places like th[at]
12	Aaron:	[Ye]ah.
13	Terry:	Umm which is, you know, you kno[w]
14	Aaron:	[Th]ose tattoos are done
15		by Ind[ian ink]
16	Gillian:	[I did th][em]
17	Aaron:	[Ye]ah
18	Terry:	But it's not something you want to advertise yourself as (1)
19	Aaron:	Right.

[29:58]

Like Anne, Terry stutters rarely. While Anne uses slightly more subtle strategies to question Aaron's story, by suggesting his hoodie makes him look suspicious, Terry is more straightforward, concluding from his tattoos that Aaron has been incarcerated. At line five, Aaron tries to respond appropriately to Terry. But Terry does not have the same timing as Anne, waiting a noticeable amount of time before speaking again. He also unintentionally insults Gillian, who drew the tattoos. Aaron is on the defensive, quick to point out that the tattoos are not real. Gillian comes to his aid in line sixteen, interrupting Aaron to take credit (or blame). However, Terry sticks to his line that others will judge Aaron by his appearance. Aaron hesitates before he responds, indicating less of a rapport with Terry than with Anne.

So far, the film has demonstrated how rhythm and a common focus can develop. At first, Aaron's talk is disjointed and incoherent, with little response from anyone else. As Anne warms up and begins to engage with him, his speech relaxes and their dialogue takes on a rhythmic tone. At this point in the conference there is a steady rhythm between Anne and Aaron. Gillian is silent, but she is closely following events, leaning forward and intensely watching. Terry's words, tone, face, and body indicate that he has resisted engagement in the interaction.

Emotional Turning Point

After thirty-five minutes Mark turns to Gillian and asks her to describe the events from her perspective.

[35:35]

1 **Gillian:** Iu::gh (1.5) I have tuh start f:: I know exactly where you are coming

2   from ((looking at Anne and nodding)) I'll explain why in a minute. . .

3   And I understand...why the both of yous ((moves gaze Terry and

4   nodding)) is still looking at Aaron, and the way he looks the way he

5   dresses the way he does his hair ((moves gaze to Aaron, and then

6   returns to Anne and Terry)). And still saying, yeah, he's one of them

7   people. He done it to get himself a quick bit of cash to get himself

8   sommin he doesn't even need. Ninety percent of the time drugs, right?

9   Um, me myself I'm, I've been to college, university, I've worked in

10   banks...I had a time in my life where I had a breakdown. (1) which is

11   why I...my doctor advised me not to work. I can't work with the

12   medication I'm taking. ((deep breath, looks up)) umm the hehehe he is

13   telling the truth at the time that I hadn't eaten for four days, before... he

14   doesn't I do not condone it at all what he done to you. I'm not trying to

15   defend him in anyway all I'm trying to explain...what happened he

16   didn't come up and just take it for drugs or anything...like that. The

17   umm he was...The police actually rang my mum, who then rang me at

18   eleven o'clock that night because they were too scared to tell me

19   ((crying)) because they were too frightened bout what I would do to

20   myself ((deep breath)) (2) that he'd been arrested and for what he'd

21   been arrested for ((glances in anger toward Aaron)). (1) so I

22   travelled. Half eleven at night I walked from Stamford Hill to Stoke

23   Newigton? With the baby? Not knowin what I was goin down to find? I

24   honestly thought, something could happen to him. ((points to herself,

25   then to him)). Because he's never _ever_ been in trouble with the police

26   before. He never…I understand what your sayin about the tattoos but

27   that's…Aaron actually does drawings for tattoo artists…and I, I like go

28   to work tattoos I've got…but mine, mine have to be outta the way for

29   when I wear uh a shirt or something they can't be seen. Eh…so…I've

30   done tattoos…so the way he does look it does sort of come across as he

31   uhh if ughhhas the _worst_ person in the world. ((Sigh)) but he aint he will

32   do _anything._ ((deep breath, moved hand to head)). Like I said ((softly,

33   under her breath)) sorry I'm getting jibbery. _like_ I say…I sat until they

34   uh they bailed him from the police station. ((deep breath in)) and they

35   sent him home from there. And then ((crying face)) I have paid for it

36   every bit as much as what he has. Everything that he has gone through

37   …I've gone through. Everything he's done, and he knows this. He get

38   this off me _every. single. day._ I tell him. Everything. Because he had

39   that minute of stupidity. That's affected your life. I I know you're just

40   saying that it's just your passport that its affected. But I know I I had a a

41   black man.. come up to me in the street in Dalston. And he followed me

42   from the post office, the police said. And he'd seen me put the money in

43   my jean jacket pocket. _He_ attacked _me._ And I fought him back. Now he

44   cut all my face, scratched all my face up wwhhen he couldn't get the

45   money from me he picked my baby's buggy up. My baby was in the

46   buggy ((crying)). And he smashed that buggy right over the street, with

47   the baby in the buggy…to get my <u>coat</u> from me. And ((looks at Aaron))

48   <u>He</u> knows this. You know, he knows the pain and everything I went

49   through. And now I'm frightened to put the baby in the buggy? Djya n

50   case someone grabs the buggy again and hurts him again. You know?

51   Mmm and he knows this ((looks at Aaron)). He's…<u>not</u>…<u>that</u>…<u>type</u>

52   …of person.

[39:35]

Certain aspects of her monologue, either intentionally or unintentionally, work to make her the centre of attention. In earlier sections, Aaron and Anne focus on each other, but for the most part they ignore their partners. Gillian, on the other hand, makes contact with everyone in the room as she talks (lines three to six). Unlike her husband, she speaks in full sentences with few stutters. Her large eyes look straight at whomever she is speaking to. She also tries to inhabit Anne and Terry's perspective at the beginning, indicating that she agrees he looks like a criminal (line three). She does this again by volunteering that she has been to college and worked in a bank, and understands their middle class values (lines nine to ten). These first eleven lines act as a preface to her story, positioning her to be on the same footing as Anne and Terry. Having done that, she takes a deep breath and moves on to the events surrounding Aaron's robbery.

In this four minute monologue, no one interrupts her, but she does not lose her momentum. She goes on to speak for about half an hour, with few interruptions or interjections from other conference participants. As she describes hearing of Aaron's arrest, her face and voice break into a cry. When she looks at Anne, her lower lips move down and outwards into a trembling frown, her lower eyelids tense up on the inside, and her eyebrows rise. However, she also has a fear crease in the middle of her brow. Her account of the night of the robbery continues until line twenty-five, where she changes focus from the facts of the robbery to a defence of Aaron's character. She goes on a brief tangent until line thirty-three, excusing and justifying Aaron's tattoos. No one interrupts her, but she recovers herself, apologizing for 'jibbering'. She then moves back to the account and finishes the story by line thirty-five.

Gillian hints at the beginning that she has a unique perspective that allows her to empathize with Anne, one that she will 'explain…in a minute'. She does not relate her own story of victimization until line forty, but we see a foreshadowing of this in line nineteen when her initial expression of sadness/fear is replaced by one of anger and disgust as she looks at Aaron and explains how upset she was to find out what he had done. As she glances at him, her eyes harden and her brow lowers slightly. She develops two vertical 'disgust lines' on both sides of her nose pointing down towards her mouth. Her mouth, while still in a frown, is different from her sadness frown in the previous figure. Her upper lip is raised in a snarl. As she looks at Aaron, it is as if she is seeing her own mugger.

Gillian's anger at Aaron further aligns her with Anne and Terry. She has gained their esteem and become the focus of their attention. In the next few lines she privileges her status of a victim above Anne when she says in line thirty-nine, 'I know you're just saying that it's just your passport that it's affected.' Her use of the word 'just' twice in this sentence belittles Anne's own victimization compared to hers. In fact, Anne never said it was 'just her passport' that was stolen. Instead, she emphasized how harmful it was to lose her passport. In describing her own mugging, Gillian also makes a point of mentioning that her robber was a black man. This seemingly needless inclusion of race in her story draws status boundaries between Aaron and a 'real' criminal element, perhaps suggesting that, in her mind, her victimization is more serious. Whether or not these are intentional strategies, she is successfully absorbing both Anne and Terry into her monologue.

As Gillian speaks, the camera lingers for a few seconds on Terry. Earlier, Terry was not focused or entrained. He was sighing and looking around the room. Here, his head is still and his eyes are focused. While his lips remain sloping downwards, he has lost the tension around his mouth. His cheeks are also more relaxed. As Gillian speaks, he very slowly nods his head. His head is tilted slightly to the left, instead of staring straight on. All of this has the effect of softening his stance and making him appear more engaged. Gillian has brought Terry into the interaction and his face appears sympathetic and caring. The camera quickly pans to Anne and Aaron and their eyes are riveted on her.

Terry is seduced by Gillian's words, and makes this clear. Over an hour into the conference, the group begins to discuss what Aaron

Figure 4.4 Focus

can do to repair the harm caused by his offence. Terry turns towards Aaron and volunteers.

1 **Terry:** ((deep audible breath)) Well, you don't have much money, and you <u>may</u>

2 go to jail on Monday, (1) but you're a very lucky bloke. (4) ((softly)) and

3 I think you know why I'm saying that. (17) ((he looks straight ahead at

4 Aaron, not blinking. Gillian wipes her eyes with a tissue and sniffs))

At this point, Gillian has set the rhythm and the tone of the conference, with the encouragement of the others. While Terry was sceptical and disengaged at the beginning, he becomes enraptured by Gillian's story. This is Terry's emotional high point. During the seventeen second pause his eyes begin to water. It is the longest pause in the conference and is only interrupted by Gillian sniffing and blowing her nose.

Gillian's monologue proves to be a turning point. She is the most emotional and expressive of all the participants and she has entrained Terry and subverted Anne's status as victim. The effects of this are twofold. First, she becomes the object of their mutual focus of attention. The conference rhythm revolves around her. Secondly, her words and emotions soften the perspectives of Anne and Terry, and make them less likely to challenge Aaron. She moves the conversation away from Anne's and Terry's scepticism about Aaron to a discussion about her and her family's victimization. Although Anne and Terry may still have cynical feelings towards Aaron, they do not bring them up again.

Balance

There are two ways of interpreting Gillian's role. First, she can be seen as a positive force, bringing the group together. Her words and tears create the collective effervescence that leads to a successful interaction ritual. Or, she can be seen as an emotional manipulator, playing to Anne and Terry's sympathies. From the latter perspective, her emotional outbreaks and her repeated references to her own victimization raise her and Aaron's status while diminishing the status of Anne and Terry. Indeed, Anne goes to great lengths to recover her lost status and to gain footing. Gillian explains that she and Aaron both have body art, but she covers hers for her job. Anne interrupts her.

[42:35]

1 **Gillian**: So:, I have to have mine wher::e, if I go into an office I can't be going

2 into an office with my tattoos and piercings showing. And,

3 basic[ally, I I]

4 **Anne**: [Whhe w]e have, we've got four kids, kay? The oldest is twenty

5 four, the youngest is eighteen. They all went to school, inner city school,

6 because we we're old fashioned socialists and we believe in equality. So

7 we send ours to the same schools as everybody else. ((gesturing with her

8 hands, scratches face)). Um::, we've got, our kids have got, we've got

9 one guy who's a friend of one of em, who's known as Pinhead ((looks

10 pointedly at Gillian and raises her eyebrows)) (2)....And what he does

11 is that he does tattooing. So...we...you know one of our sons is an art

12 student. And an awful lot of his friends look...pretty freaky. (1) We're

13 not, we we don't judge you by your appearance without stopping

14 to think. I mean obviously, when what you were doing at that moment,

15   when I first clapped eyes on you, made me perceive your appearance as

16   being part…part of a stereotype. But we don't _really_ see people in

17   stereotypes that coldly. Umm you know.. .

[43:44]

Anne uses a number of strategies above to defend herself against Gillian. While her speech is clear, she struggles more for her words, with more frequent stutters and pauses than earlier. She draws on her children's experiences to raise her own status, explaining that their children have a tattoo-artist friend with an alternative appearance, stuttering over whether Pinhead is her friend or her children's friend. She offers the fact that her son is an art student to gain footing and appear less judgmental.

Anne tries to make clear in this passage that she and Terry do not judge Aaron by his appearance. This contradicts what both she and her husband said earlier about his appearance. She is back-pedalling, working to appease both Gillian and Aaron. Her speech and actions in this excerpt give Gillian the upper hand.

These few minutes of the conference are also important because they show Aaron in a different light. As Gillian continues speaking, she begins to cry harder. Mark hands her a tissue to wipe her running nose. She struggles for a moment to both wipe her nose and hold her sleeping baby. Aaron leans over and takes the sleeping baby out of her lap. The camera zooms out and we see Aaron cradling his son while Gillian continues addressing Anne and Terry through her tears. Aaron holds his sleeping son in his arms, gently stroking his head. This image (whether intentional or not) further raises Aaron's status, displaying him in a domestic light that is much different to the image of a hooded mugger.

The exchanges between Gillian and Anne reveal a more critical interpretation of the conference. On the one hand, the conference has all of the ingredients of a successful interaction. The participants develop a rhythm and a shared focus of attention. However, instead of focusing attention on the robbery or Anne's victimization, Gillian has become the centre of the interaction. One cannot analyse Gillian's motivation with this data. We do not know whether she was being manipulative or simply expressing genuine emotion. From a ritual perspective, this does not really matter. Intentions may, or may not, be genuine, but the end result is four people equally engrossed in the interaction, expressing some kind of solidarity. This is the mark of a successful interaction.

Solidarity and Symbolic Reparation

Whether or not Gillian and Aaron use strategies to gain the upper hand does not affect the general rhythmic tone. Anne and Terry are responsive to both Gillian and Aaron. All of the participants are rhythmically entrained with each other, engaging each other in turn-taking conversation and sharing a mutual focus of attention. An examination of both their facial expressions and demeanour and discourse in the final moments of the conference reveals group solidarity.

In an interaction ritual, solidarity is loosely defined as a feeling of group membership and closeness (Collins, 2004). It is a direct result of the collective effervescence developed through a rhythmic and entrained interaction. This feeling of togetherness manifests itself in instances where group members share an identity, or cooperate together. This can also be externalized by instances of sustained eye contact, turn-taking, laughing, crying, or touching.

Following the emotional high point of the interaction, the conference moves to the final stage, where the group collectively decides on the positive steps Aaron can take to repair the harm caused by the offence. Anne and Terry are both very clear that they want Aaron to 'get his life together'—get a job, take care of his wife and child. Mark asks Gillian what she would like to see happen. While echoing Anne and Terry's sentiments, her request is more personal.

[70:18]

1 **Gillian:** I. (3)I. I. I'll be honest with the both of yous. And…as far as the

2   situations I'm sitting in now I'm at my final straw. So if Aaron doesn't

3   go to prison on Monday, if he doesn't start work in the first week of the

4   new year than he won't…be…with me, and he <u>knows</u> this. Cus

5   I can't keep putting…not myself, h[im] ((pointing to baby)).=

6 **Anne:**   [mm]mm::

7 **Gillian:** =I can't keep putting him through it. N::uun::, you know yourself,

8   as a mo[ther]

9 **Anne:**   [Mmm]hhm ((nodding))

10 **Gillian:**   I can::'t.

11 **Anne:**   He <u>has to come first</u>.

12 **Gillian:**   Yeah. He has to come firs[t.]

13 **Anne:**   [mm]mm

14 **Gillian:**   And if that means Aaron leavin my life then yeah that does mean it

15   and he knows yeaah he [knows i]t.

16 **Anne:**   [mmmm]

17 **Gillian:**   I won't think twice about looking ba[ck.]

18 **Anne:**   [mm]m

[71:06]

Not only is their conversation full of appropriate turn-taking conventions and back channel cues, but they are also relating to each other as mothers with similar identities. They experience a moment in which they share the same priorities. Anne encourages Gillian, who becomes more and more adamant about her intentions to leave Aaron if he does not change. This is a moment of intense, female-centred solidarity.

A few minutes later Gillian explains that Aaron has sold a few of his drawings to tattoo artists. This exchange is unique because all four of them give input. Terry even offers Aaron advice on how to look better before the judge.

1 **Gillian:**   I've got, em:::, I've got quite a few tattoos. But…three of them are

2   actually Aaron's dra[wing]s

3 **Anne:**   [mmm]mm

4 **Gillian:**   I've took them to a professional shop and had them d[one]=

5 **Anne:**   [mmm]

6 **Gillian:**   =professional. They they, what they normally say is, that if he gives

7   them the draw[ing]=

8 **Anne:**   [mmm]

9 **Gillian:**   =[a]nd then they do the tattoo che[ap=

10 **Anne:**   [mmmm]

11 **Gillian:**   =an]d they give him a coupla pou[nd=

12 **Anne:**   [Mmm]

13 **Gillian:**   =For doin[g it].

14 **Terry:**   [mm][mm]

15 **Anne:**   [mm][mm]

16 **Gillian:**   [But] hehehe, he's quite [good.]

17 **Anne:**   [mmm]

18 **Gillian:**   When he puts his mind to thin[gs.]

19 **Terry:**   [I m]ean if you <u>are</u> going to present

20   a dossie[r,]=

21 **Aaron:**   [Ye][aaah]

22 **Terry:**   =[To the judge, on Mond[ay]=

23 **Aaron:**   [Yeaah]

24 **Terry:**   =[It] might be quite useful, to produce a portfolio of some of your work.

25   Two reasons, one it

26   shows that you've got some of the sk[ill]=

27 **Aaron:**   [Yeah]

28 **Terry:**   =And two it it in a way <u>justi</u>fies your having your own tattoo[s]

29 **Aaron:**   [Y][eah]

30 **Anne:**   [Mmm]

31 **Gillian:**   [Mmm]

32 **Terry:**   Yeah?

33 **Aaron:**   Yeah.

34 **Terry:**   Um::::: so that might be a bit helpful to you

The usual externalizations of solidarity such as smiling and touching follow. At the end of the conference, as they are getting ready to leave, Anne puts out her hand for Aaron to shake. He takes it and they smile. This moment illustrates a kind of solidarity between these two. Compare Anne's smile to her Pan-Am smile in Figure 4.1. Here, she is smiling with her whole face, not just her mouth. Aaron, too, has a full faced smile, and his anxiety wrinkles are gone from his brow. This is the only shot of him in the entire video with a smooth forehead. It has taken a while to get to this point, but these two seem glad to be shaking hands.

Figure 4.5 Solidarity

Retzinger and Scheff (1996) have argued that symbolic reparation is more important in restorative justice than material reparation. Aaron expresses remorse from the beginning of the conference, and apologizes multiple times. By all accounts he appears genuine, and Anne accepts his apology. Terry starts out more suspicious of Aaron, but by the end of the conference he too seems invested in a positive outcome. There is a final moment of symbolic reparation at the end when they break for tea and biscuits. The others have left the circle for tea, but Gillian remains seated tending to her son. Terry comes over and offers a chocolate biscuit to the child. The room falls silent while everyone watches the child tentatively grasp the biscuit. It is as if the biscuit is a peace offering from Terry: he may not yet forgive, but this offering symbolizes his acceptance of them. This moment feels meaningful, more so than when they sign the outcome agreement.

Do Motivations Matter?

I suggested earlier that we cannot tell whether Gillian is expressing heartfelt emotion or is entering into a status contest with the victim. The point I make is that it doesn't matter what Gillian is intending, we will never truly know, even if we ask her. What we do know is what we observe, which is a sustained rhythmic engagement between all participants and overt verbal and bodily displays of solidarity suggesting that this is a successful interaction ritual. Intentions and motivations take a back seat to the ritual solidarity on display.

This theme also comes out in my interviews with facilitators in Chapters Five and Six. They suggest that some of the best conferences are the ones where the participants did not have the 'right' motivations going into it. Such conferences are particularly effective as the emotional 'turning points' can be so pronounced. On the other hand, conferences with dubious victims or cynical offenders could also backfire, embodying little restoration or justice. My position in reading conference dynamics is founded on exactly this point: motivations do not determine success in restorative justice. Instead, 'success' is in the ability of the conference to take on elements of a successful interaction ritual, carefully guided by the facilitator to produce rhythmic dialogue, emotional entrainment, a balance of power and status, and identifiable emotional 'turning points'. This leads to group solidarity in the short-term, and perhaps emotional energy and reduced offending in the long-term.

Emotional Energy

Emotional energy is one of the positive outcomes of successful interaction rituals. It is related to, and stems from, solidarity and is the individual level feeling that arises out of the group state. Emotional energy is the generalized state of well-being that follows on from high solidarity interaction. It is a sense of elation that can be felt in the air and seen on people's faces—they look relaxed, happy, and at ease.

The feeling of emotional energy is something an individual takes away from a group interaction. It is felt in the moments, hours, or even days following the interaction ritual. In this case, the filmmakers conducted a brief exit interview with each participant after the conference, asking them general questions about how they thought it went. These interviews can provide insight into their emotional states after the conference. Additionally, by examining how they talk about what they just experienced, one can triangulate what we observed in the conference with what participants say in the interview. This acts as a useful confirmation, or disconfirmation, of the observed emotions.

When asked by the filmmakers what they thought about the conference, the positive emotions of solidarity observed in the previous image spill out of the conference room into the corridor. Anne and Terry are standing in the corridor, with their coats on, ready to leave. The cameraman asks how they thought the conference went. Anne looks at Terry and he responds:

Terry: ((Sigh)) ((smiling and laughing)). It was, it was ammAAzing. I've been through not dissimilar experiences but I wouldnta expected…. Ahhm:::….the sort of, reaction, particularly from Gillian, his wife. You know I thought that was…that was very impressive…ahhm::…and if he lets her down, he deserves to have his head taken off.

Before he speaks, he takes a deep breath and sighs. As he exhales, his shoulders drop into a relaxed position. He labels the conference amazing, a smile crosses his face, and he shakes his head in disbelief. This is the only time his smile is caught on video. When he says the last two lines about Gillian, he looks straight into the camera, raises his eyebrows, and shakes his head. His answer and his demeanour suggest heightened emotional energy.

Gillian also shares a high level of emotional energy after the conference. She and Aaron are interviewed outside the building as they are leaving to go home. As they take a moment to smoke a cigarette together, they explain how surprised and pleased they were by Anne and Terry.

Gillian: I was surpri:::sed cus you know. I felt all awkward when you went to uh::::…you had to write the things out? And I felt awkward then, but dj::: <u>she</u> started talking ((smiles and shakes her head)) you know? It's like she…I'm <u>pleased</u> cuz she…it's like she understands ((large, toothy grin)).

Gillian is also talking in a much more relaxed voice. A smile doesn't leave her face the whole time, and she is gesturing animatedly. She feels a genuine connection to Anne. She points to an 'awkward' moment of the conference, when they all had to sign the outcome agreement (again a sign that this may not be a meaningful symbol). She shows gratitude to Anne for rescuing the embarrassing moment by changing the subject and talking to her. To Gillian, this is a sign that Anne understands and respects her.

All of the conference participants exhibit signs of positive emotional energy. Compared to the earlier images of them, they are more relaxed and happy. They smile as they talk; animatedly report how pleased they are; and are buzzing with goodwill.

Discussion

This conference fits a model of a successful interaction ritual. The participants become engrossed with each other over time, moving from hesitant, awkward conversation to instances of high solidarity and shared emotion. While Terry is initially resistant, there is an identifiable turning point when Gillian speaks. Although she dominates the interaction, and at times subverts Anne's status as victim, Anne and Terry respond positively, engaging in high solidarity interaction with Gillian and Aaron.

The current analysis uses systematic micro methods to show that the elements of a successful interaction ritual can be empirically observed, documented, and analysed. This advances the ritual perspective, using interaction ritual theory (Collins, 2004) to develop a micro level theory of restorative justice. Elements of the theory include:

1. *Shared focus through conversational rhythm.* Although initially disjointed, over time participants settle into a turn-taking dynamic marked by a lessening of stutters and silences. They begin to share a common focus and communicate with each other directly.
2. *Conversational and power balance.* All participants feel empowered to contribute, and no one is dominated. In this conference, Gillian talks more than anyone else, but this does not alter the balance of the conference. All participants continue to engage with each other and do not withdraw from the conversation.
3. *Turning point.* Strong expressions of emotions act as a high point for participants, providing a common focus and drawing them all into the rhythm and the flow of the interaction.
4. *Public displays of solidarity.* After a rhythm has developed, and the interaction has reached a crescendo, participants engage in high-solidarity interactions such as touching, sustained eye contact, or other elements of high-solidarity conversation.

This is not a chronological, or exhaustive, list of essential elements. The key component is the development of an interactional rhythm. The other elements contribute to, or are a result of, this rhythmic entrainment between participants. The process is dynamic, moving forwards and backwards in space and time. This analysis suggests that one can empirically isolate the components of a successful restorative justice conference and this knowledge can be used to develop strategies that maximize emotions and ensure strong rituals.

One limitation of the preceding analysis is that it only takes into account a 'successful' case. A similar analysis of 'failed' cases will strengthen, or perhaps modify, the elements of the theory. As Goffman pointed out repeatedly (Goffman, 1959, 1961, 1967), analysing how interactions fail is the best way to teach us how they work. Future research can build on this to refine the theory.

Conclusion

This conference has elements of both successful interaction ritual and emotional manipulation. Importantly, the judge in Aaron's case regarded the conference as a success. At the sentencing hearing the judge remanded the case and demanded to see the video footage of the conference. When everyone reassembled for the sentencing a few days later, he publicly remarked:

I now know more about your attitude than perhaps any other defendant…There is no reason why I shouldn't tell you that I found it a very moving experience. It was not only helpful to hear what the victim said but it was also useful to see the expression on your face and I do not believe that you were acting. Every possible indication is that you were genuinely contrite.

He proceeded to sentence Aaron to 240 hours of community service. His evocation of his own emotional reaction to the conference runs counter to ordinary courtroom dynamics, which seek to suppress emotion and encourage rational deliberation (Sherman, 2003). According to the judge, this interaction ritual was powerful enough to prevent Aaron from going to prison.

This video shows the micro workings of interaction ritual in restorative justice. It allows us to pinpoint precisely how rhythm and shared focus can develop, and how solidarity and positive emotions are expressed. This analysis has given us a model of how a restorative justice conference can be a transformative, and ritually successful event. It provides a systematic and rigorous approach to uncover how restorative justice 'works'. The approach and methodology developed here can be used to examine future conferences to develop a comprehensive theory of restorative justice interactions.

5

Preparing for Powerful Rituals

Restorative justice encounters do not begin the moment the participants enter the room. Rather, they are the culmination of a long build-up of emotions, interactions, and, sometimes delicate, negotiations that have been carefully thought through and choreographed by the facilitator. This chapter explores what goes into creating the conditions under which successful restorative justice outcomes can be observed.

Interviews with facilitators are a particularly instructive way of identifying the key elements that go into making a conference happen. As described in Chapter Three, the facilitators in this study were asked to identify their 'best', 'worst', and 'typical' conference. Once they had chosen their cases, we examined their files in-depth, discussing all the events and activities surrounding the organization of the conference as well as the actual encounter. Interviews were semi-structured and we discussed each case for about two hours. Facilitators are trained to be attuned to group-level dynamics and their accounts were detailed and precise. This approach to analysing ritual dynamics is consistent with the techniques laid out in the theory of interaction ritual chains (Collins, 2004: 97).

The definition of 'success' can be slippery. I purposely was loose in my request that the facilitators nominate their 'successes' and 'failures'. I wanted to see how they defined success, and how components of interaction ritual map onto this definition. All facilitators categorized their 'best' conferences as being the most emotionally intense, and their worst as either being emotionally flat, or very intense for one party but not the other. Ritual success is only one of many possible definitions of success in restorative justice. Other commonly used measures include victim and offender satisfaction, procedural fairness, and reoffending. My aim in looking at the ritual dynamics of the conference is to suggest that understanding these dynamics is the key to developing a sound measure of success in restorative justice. By examining in-depth what does and does not work in a restorative justice conference—and failed cases here are particularly instructive—and mapping the dynamics of the interactions within them, we can develop a model of what constitutes a successful conference.

Setting up the Encounter

Conferences in this study were organized fairly quickly as facilitators were constrained by the window between guilty plea and sentence. They often had six weeks or less to bring everybody together. Over this period they spent approximately twenty-five person-hours on each case. This included a series of preparatory meetings with the conference participants and, perhaps, visits to the prison if the offender was in custody. In their initial meetings with victim and offender, they requested the names of potential supporters. They may also have spoken to police officers involved in the case, witnesses, probation officers, care workers, psychologists, and victim support workers.

This is an important stage. The investment in time during the preparatory meetings allowed for trust to develop between the participants and the facilitator. This trust was vital to the careful and precise staging of the event. In these initial meetings, the facilitator prepared the participants for the emotions they were likely to experience during the conference. This preparatory emotional build-up would prove necessary in order to maximize the emotional intensity at the conference. Finally, the facilitators demonstrated resourcefulness and creativity to imaginatively coordinate the event, deal with anxieties and other participant concerns, and solve last minute organizational problems.

Trust Building

In order for the event to be a success, facilitators must appear honourable and trustworthy to all participants. They often have to deal with a general distrust of police by participants who assume they are 'out to get them'. In their meetings with offenders, they are non-judgmental and respectful. Their biggest danger is of coming across as a 'typical cop', at which point an offender is likely to shut down. As one facilitator put it, 'I think I was one of the very first police officers that actually treated him like a human being.' This respectful treatment of the offender allowed trust to develop and, as a result, the offender freely participated and engaged in the conference.

With victims, the facilitators are supportive and caring while, at the same time, making it clear that they require all participants, including the offender, to be treated with respect. For example, in meeting with a potential victim supporter, a facilitator recalled,

She was very typical of victims' relatives. She wanted to rip this guy's lungs out through his backside, she wanted to do all sorts of questionable things to him. And I explained to her, this guy is a human being, and maybe this will help you as well by having your say. So she said yes.

Part of trust building is knowing when to ease the pressure on potential participants. Often when an offender or victim does not consent, or consents but does not volunteer any supporters, the facilitator will back off, and wait for a few days before asking again. Facilitators feel they need to display calmness and patience so they don't appear to be 'trying to sell them something'. This strategy allows for a cooling-off period, after which facilitators report that participants can be more cooperative.

Emotional Preparatory Work

Facilitators describe a build-up of emotional intensity that takes place in the weeks, days, and minutes leading up to the event, as well as in the preliminary stages of the actual conference. For example, in his discussions with each of the participants the facilitator will encourage them to think about what effect the crime has had on them and how they will express this to those attending the conference. As the conference day approaches, and in the moments immediately preceding it, this build-up of emotions will be felt by all of the participants. One facilitator describes the way this build-up feels.

It was just like a boiling pot. It was just bubbling. It was something almost tangible. It was really weird. I wasn't prepared for it. I could just tell that there was a lot of anger, a lot of fear. I could tell that people were bursting to speak, people wanted to speak. Because I had said to him [the offender], 'This is your chance. Show this person that you are not the bag of shit that he thinks you are.' And to the victim I said, 'This is your time to explain what this person has done to your life, what he has done to you.'

For this facilitator, the pre-conference preparation, which involved encouraging participants to bring their feelings to the surface, contributed to a palpable sense of intensity in the conference.

Preliminary emotions

Offenders and victims commonly express a variety of emotions in the lead-up to, and during, the restorative justice conference: these include anger, fear, anxiety, embarrassment, and shame. It is clear these emotions may build steadily in intensity in the days and minutes prior to the conference. For victims especially, anger, often combined with fear or anxiety, is the most common emotion.

In discussions with the facilitator, victims' anger may take the form of bluster in which they may even express a desire to physically harm the offender. Although no conferences in this research resulted in actual violence, the threat of violence may have been expressed. For example, one facilitator describes his meetings with two adult sons of a victim of robbery.

> The two sons said, 'We daren't come along because, if we do, we'll kill him'…that's been said before, 'I want to kill him.' But a lot of it is just the emotionality coming out. If push came to shove, I don't think they would actually do it. They would probably get really upset and be in his face.

Another common emotion among victims and offenders is anxiety. It is rare to find a conference where at least one, or both, parties do not feel nervous going into the event. In one extreme example, an offender was so overcome with nerves as she approached the door to the conference room that she almost lost her ability to walk.

> It was incredibly emotional in that really quiet anticipating way. It was difficult to get [the offender] into the room. She only had to walk about ten yards across a landing to get into the room. And she stopped outside and her legs and knees gave way. I held onto her elbow, sort of held her up. And she supported herself on the wall. And she said, 'I don't think I can go in there.' And I said, 'We've come this far, but nobody can make you go into the room. They're all in there, waiting to hear from you.' And she said, 'No, I've come this far I'll go in …' She obviously had a last bout of energy or something from there. And she held herself up straight and walked into the room directly to her seat.

Facilitators describe a range of other physical symptoms of anxiety including shaking hands, sweating, pale skin, crying, repeatedly touching their face and head, shifting their weight from one side of the body to the other, constantly moving their hands, picking at their nails. Sometimes participants are so nervous that they are overcome with fits of laughter, as one facilitator explained: 'That kind of giggling laughter release that people have when they're trying to find something funny in something that is quite difficult.' Or, their body and demeanour changes, as was the case with one elderly victim as she approached the prison where the conference was being held.

She wasn't saying an awful lot. It was almost as if she was trying to make herself look small. She was almost like withdrawing into herself. She was obviously just very uncomfortable about the whole thing. She didn't look confident about the situation.

In another case, a victim's wife succumbed to an attack of eczema outside the prison just before going into the conference.

[Her] eczema flared, to the point where she looked like a beetroot. She was purple. She had it all over...most of her body...her nerves and the stress of attending the conference made her erupt, literally erupt. She was just purple, pink, red.

Embarrassment and shame are commonly experienced by both offenders and victims. Offenders may feel ashamed because of the remorse they feel at having to come face to face with the victim and their families, or they may be just plain sorry they got caught. They may display shame at the beginning of the conference as, for example, with two co-offenders who sat,

looking down...really unhappy. They were avoiding eye contact. They were hunched forward. And they were both saying, 'We are so stupid. So stupid', banging the arms of the chair and asking themselves, 'Why did we do this?'

Victims can blame themselves as well, especially where they believe they are savvy urbanites who should not have 'allowed themselves' to be victimized. For example, as one conference facilitator described, '[the victim] had come from South Africa where there are huge crime problems, and she fell for a trick like this in England. She was extremely upset with herself.' This sense of shame and self-blame after a seemingly random attack can be common among victims of crime.

The Role of Physical and Emotional Harm

There is some evidence that conferences involving victims who suffer ongoing harm may be more emotionally intense. Although the crimes in this study were serious enough to be dealt with in the Crown Court, many did not involve direct contact between victim and offender and did not seem to exhibit serious lasting physical and emotional harm to the victim (Angel, 2005). When selecting their best cases, however, facilitators tended to choose ones involving serious harm to the victim. This is consistent with other research on restorative justice that suggests it is most likely to be effective with more serious offences (Sherman and Strang, 2007). One example of this involved a robbery by a female crack addict.

She [the victim] had been totally devastated by this crime. She was struck over the head with a bottle and [the offender] grabbed her handbag, and struck her several times…It was a nasty robbery. [The victim] had quite a huge damage to her head. And since then she hadn't gone back to work, she wouldn't go about by herself, she hadn't even bought another handbag. Her life had been affected extraordinarily.

After the conference, the victim contacted the facilitator to report back that she bought herself a new handbag when it was over, an action that symbolized a marked improvement in her sense of safety and security.

Evidence that conferences can assist victims in dealing with their trauma (see Angel, 2005) was supported by facilitators who use a range of strategies to both build emotion prior to the event and bring it out during the conference. Indeed their express aim, they reported, was to maximize the expression of these emotional displays through the build-up of anxiety, anger, and shame in the lead-up to the conference. In their opinion this was more likely to occur in cases where the victim was experiencing identifiable and ongoing harm.

These findings suggest that serious harm, coupled with powerful emotional responses, is a component of successful restorative justice conferences. This focus on bringing emotions to the surface, as well as maximizing their expression, is in contrast to other social rituals such as court hearings, where individuals are expected to contain their emotions, avoid conflict, or minimize the expression of feelings. Even more significantly, it would appear that with less serious offences the emotions may not be sufficiently strong to enable a successful ritual. In short, the stronger the emotions, whether they be positive or negative, the better the conference.

Imaginative Problem Solving

There is often a complicated staging process to get these conferences off the ground. First, a time and date has to be found within a brief window that can accommodate everyone. On the day of the conference participants are likely to be on edge and disaster can strike if the timing is not right. This is especially true when conferences are held in prison, where the victim and offender supporters often have to wait together to be let into the prison, then wait together again in the conference room for the offender to be brought in from the cells. In these cases, the facilitator often relies on support staff to smooth the entry into the conference room.

For example, in the manslaughter case discussed in Chapter One, the prison was located in the countryside a four hour train ride from the homes of the offenders' supporters and the victim and her supporters. Trains ran infrequently and there was only one train that would arrive in time. The facilitator anticipated that everyone would be on edge and that the slightest negative experience could ruin the planned event. Because of this, he enlisted the help of an additional facilitator, as well as a member of the support staff, to make sure everyone's attention was sufficiently diverted from the task at hand.

The facilitator examined the train station in advance and picked out separate meeting spots for the different parties. He made sure that they were waiting at different ends of the platform for the train to arrive, and reserved seats on opposite ends of the train. The act of separating the parties took on symbolic meaning after the conference when everybody decided to travel home on the train together.

There can be further problems dealing with prisons whose staff may not be experienced in dealing with these kinds of activities. While many conferences run smoothly and on time, there can be last minute potential disasters, such as participants forgetting the necessary identification to enter the prison, people arriving late and not being allowed in, or staff on duty not being aware of a scheduled conference and refusing to bring the offender out from his cell. For example, in a typical conference held in a prison,

R: We had a hell of a job of getting in because it was one of those things where nobody knew anything about it. The only contact that I had, who arranged everything, wasn't there on that day and so I had a hell of a job trying to get in. Which took a lot of time. I always find it very difficult that you have these people who are potentially in conflict. You have the mother of the defendant there with the victim and her daughter. So you have got these people who really don't want to be together, but they are forced together waiting to get in. Somebody was outside sitting with them and I was just hoping that we would get ahold of somebody. And eventually we did, and we got in. But it was a long wait and quite hard job to get into the prison.

I: How long were you waiting?

R: Maybe half an hour with people denying all knowledge of this [the conference room booking and the release of the prisoner]. No one knew anything about it, like it hadn't been arranged.

This is typical of what facilitators might face. Regardless of what arises, they must continue to project an aura of calmness and control to ease the anxiety or impatience of the participants, while they find ways to address any unanticipated problems.

Inside the Conference

Privacy, group assembly, and the development of rhythm through a mutual focus of attention and shared mood are the key ingredients to a successful ritual. In the interviews, which probed for the presence, or absence, of these elements in each of the facilitators' three selected conferences, some clear distinctions between the ingredients of successes and failures were apparent. Three ingredients consistent with Collin's interaction ritual model included face-to-face co-presence, privacy, and rhythm (see Table 5.1). In addition, five further ingredients were identified that help explain the variations between conferences: the quality of the space, the conversational balance, an identifiable turning point in the interaction (the emotional 'high' point), the presence of offender supporters, and the presence of victim supporters (see Appendix 2 for details of how these items were measured and coded).

As Table 5.1 shows, there is a clear distinction between successful and failed conferences, and this will be discussed further. The most striking distinctions concerned the development of a conversational and interaction rhythm, conversational balance, turning point, and the presence of supporters.

Table 5.1 Ritual Ingredients by Conference Type

	Successes (n = 9)	Typical (n = 6)	Failures (n = 9)
Face-to-face	9 (100%)	6 (100%)	9 (100%)
Privacy	9 (100)	5 (83)	8 (89)
Rhythm	8 (89)	5 (83)	0 (0)
Adequate space	7 (78)	4 (67)	6 (67)
Balance	9 (100)	6 (100)	6 (67)
Turning point	9 (100)	1 (17)	0 (0)
Offender supporters	8 (89)	4 (67)	6 (67)
Victim supporters	9 (100)	3 (50)	4 (44)

Choreographing the Space

Facilitators emphasize the importance of the placement of people around the circle, particularly in terms of minimizing conflict and creating safety while (paradoxically) at the same time maximizing the opportunities for eye contact and confrontation. Before a conference, they carefully plan where each participant will sit. For example, they make sure the offender and victim are immediately surrounded by those expected to be most supportive of them. In an attempt to create a sense of safety and security, they also identify individuals who can act as 'buffers' between the offender and victim parties such as when, in one case, a facilitator explained how they chose to place a female drugs worker between the victim's and the offender's parties because she was the most 'neutral'. For this reason, they may place the person they deem the most vulnerable—a particularly traumatized or upset victim for instance—next to them for support. Other times they may place the most volatile person next to them so they can 'control' them.

Facilitators assess what they know about each party when deciding where they should sit. In describing the rationale for the seating arrangement shown in Figure 5.1, the facilitator said that because of the victim's anxiety he wanted to 'have her flanked by her daughters' so she would feel supported and comforted by them. He also knew from previous meetings that the offender's mother was terrified of confronting the victim so he placed her next to himself 'in case she needed support from me'. He also did not want

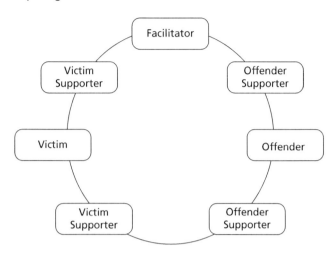

Figure 5.1 Typical Seating Arrangement

the offender to sit directly next to anyone from the victim's party so he made the offender's brother the buffer between the two parties.

While the arrangement of the circle and the placement of buffers is an important consideration for facilitators, there were instances where conference participants consciously manipulated the space to create an imbalance. In one case, for example, an exceptionally hostile victim and her family picked up the chairs, which were arranged in a circle, and moved them out of the circle and away from the offender and his family (see Figure 5.2).

First of all, it wasn't a circle. I arranged the chairs in a circle…And the mother and her daughters picked up the chairs and went off at an angle, sort of forty-five degrees to me in a straight line. So I had a semi-circle, and then a straight line. They arranged that themselves. And they distanced themselves from the offender…I thought, 'Here we go, it can only get worse.' So I said, 'It would help if we sat in a circle, for the benefit of everybody. So we can all hear what everybody else is saying.' And mum said, 'I don't want to get any closer than this.' And that's how things started.

The victims rearranged the space to demonstrate their control of the situation and attitude to the offender. In disrupting the carefully managed placing of the seats, they not only created a physical imbalance, but also sent a signal to both the offender and his supporters about how the interaction was likely to be played out.

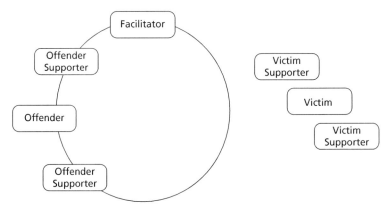

Figure 5.2 Manipulated Seating Arrangement

Other challenges to creating a suitable space include room size, lighting, temperature, and privacy. This is a particular challenge in prisons, where the rooms are not purpose built for such encounters. For example, conferences in this study were held in a range of spaces, including prison classrooms, corridors, chapels, interview rooms, and even a governor's office. Sometimes prison officers insisted on being present, sometimes they insisted on keeping a prisoner shackled. Interview rooms meant for two to three people would sometimes accommodate six or seven chairs, so that participants had to sit with their knees touching. People might walk in and out of the room to use a vending machine or a photocopier. In one instance, there was construction work directly outside an open window, with a constant barrage of machines running during the conference.

The majority of the non-custody conferences were held in a specially designed set of rooms. Separate smaller rooms were used as waiting areas for the victim's side and the offender's side. Usually the victim and their supporters were brought into the room first and made to feel comfortable, followed by the offender and their supporters.

Regardless of the location, facilitators did their best to create a safe and welcoming space for all participants. They put significant thought into their seating arrangements, everyone was greeted with a friendly smile and a cup of tea, and the group was able to proceed quickly.

Rhythm and Entrainment

I think there comes a point, this is usually after the offender has said whatever he's got to say, and the victim will either start in there by asking questions or they will say their piece and then they will ask a question. Or someone else will chip in a question at some point after the introduction. And then the conference can just take on the life of its own. [Conference Facilitator]

A key ingredient in a successful interaction ritual is the development of rhythmic entrainment between the participants. In this context, rhythm refers to the linguistic and bodily synchronization of the interaction. People follow turn-taking rules, respect and encourage each other, and develop a flow in their interaction. Entrainment is a sense of mutual engagement and shared mood. As a rhythm develops, participants become focused on the same object.

While none of the facilitators' failed conferences had this characteristic, they all described how a rhythm developed between participants in every one of their successful conferences. It develops over time and is observed when people engage in typical rules of conversation: taking turns to speak, maintaining appropriate eye contact, making an effort to fill gaps and silences in the conversation, and responding appropriately to questions. Conferences may start out fragmented, with people reluctant to speak and with the facilitator having to work hard to draw people out, but as it progresses the nerves slowly dissipate and a rhythm develops. This is what allows the victim, offender, and their families to have a productive conference.

In an interview with a young man who was participating because of a burglary he committed, he described the early stages of his conference and what precipitated a change of rhythm.

R: At first they [the victims] didn't understand because I wasn't talking. So they kinda got a bit angry. Not angry, but didn't know why they were bothering. I just sat there. I wanted to have words, but I just couldn't say anything.

I: So you think they were angry at you towards the beginning?

R: Yeah, 'cos it was like I wasn't paying attention, or even caring. Then my brother had to stand up and say something...but at the end of it I told them what I was really thinking. It was good.

Whether due to anxiety or fear, initially the young man felt unable to speak in the conference. It continued in a disjointed manner: participants questioned him and received no response. The victims, who assumed he was being uncooperative, interpreted this negatively and were becoming increasingly frustrated. Only when the young man's brother dramatically stood up and confronted him did a transitional moment occur. Thereafter, he was able to take part in the dialogue and this contributed to what he judged to be a successful conference.

Another offender explicitly noted how the conference settled into a rhythm where he and the victim focused on communicating their shared feelings and addressing the harm.

I: Were you nervous?

R: A bit. A little bit. As the conversation starts flowing, you tend to sort of like, I don't know, the nervousness tends to start to go away a little bit, doesn't it? Start getting to know each other in that sense, right? And, he was putting questions to me, I was putting questions to him, and it went as it should have, in that way. You know, there was no abusing or anything like that, you know?

Conferences may at first lack continuity, with long pauses and unnatural silences, but over time a rhythm emerges and participants develop a mutual focus of attention.

Facilitators are trained to use unnatural silences to motivate people to speak, but even they report that silences can become 'unbearable', and they feel almost overwhelmed by a desire to start a conversation going. They know that if they are feeling uncomfortable, however, the other participants are likely to be feeling similarly anxious and embarrassed and, if they wait, someone will eventually attempt to break the suspense by speaking. These can be the most revealing moments of a conference, and are often referred to as a 'turning point'.

From the participants' point of view, it may seem like the facilitator is not doing much: for example, in one case the offender reported that the facilitator 'wasn't really involved in it too much. He obviously made the introductions and all that, and then he didn't do much of the talking.' From the facilitator's perspective, on the other hand, he was working hard to keep track of everything that was going on around him, noting who was feeling excluded or overwhelmed, and subtly encouraging others to do the work.

In another example, a facilitator described how a long silence led to a particularly powerful moment of engagement. It was in a conference where the offender had sliced the victim with a machete during the course of a robbery. At one point, the victim lifted his shirt to reveal the deep scars caused by the machete attack. There was a fifteen to twenty second pause as everyone looked in horror at the scarring. The offender looked startled and slightly panicked, he glanced around the circle and then looked at the facilitator, they locked eyes for a moment and the facilitator raised his eyes 'in a friendly way'. The offender then turned to the victim and said, 'I would do anything to be forgiven for what I've done.' Looking back, the facilitator recalled,

When there is a pause people tend to look to the facilitator, as if to say 'What are you going to do now?' But again I explained to them that there will be pauses where I stare at you, or when I look away…I always say to people, you will be surprised by what you hear, but you will be more surprised by what you say. And it's always true.

While silences may be positive in the sense that they can encourage people to speak, they can also be damaging if no one steps up to fill the gap. Such conferences present the biggest challenge to facilitators because they are forced into the role of inquisitor: asking leading questions and trying to prompt people to speak. When this happens, conversations become fragmented, with participants communicating through the facilitator rather than directly with each other, and this makes it difficult, if not impossible, to develop rhythm between the parties. This can be seen in the failed conference described in Chapter One in which the offender had few English language skills and may not have understood why he was present. The other participants were an interpreter, and the victim who had reluctantly agreed to attend.

It was hard. The conference lasted for fifty-five minutes, but I had to do a lot of interrupting, and use a lot of leading questions to get them talking and to give them ideas of what to say. Having somebody there that doesn't understand English, I can't say that the victim can be very satisfied with what he is getting.

With the interpreter present, the victim and offender never addressed each other directly, and never developed a turn-taking rhythm. This may have been due to inadequate interpreting, or a lack of briefings to the participants on how to work with the interpreter. But it seems likely that the mediated nature of talk in this instance presented an extra challenge to the development of a conversational rhythm. According to the facilitator, the conference failed to develop any 'flow' and, in his opinion, was a 'complete waste of time'.

Balance of Emotions and Power

In order for a rhythm and mutual focus of attention to develop, there needs to be a balance of emotions and power. This can be observed at a number of levels: most obviously through the amount of speaking each party does or, more subtly, through acts of domination or repression such as interruptions or the ignoring of input. This is most clearly demonstrated through disruptions and imbalances. If one party consistently violates turn-taking rules and dominates the interaction, this may lead to a harmful imbalance. And while the expressions of emotions are a necessary and important part of the interaction, such imbalance can have a negative and counter-productive effect.

In the previous example, no rhythm developed and the participants did not engage in the process. This resulted in a relatively 'flat' conference which, while doing no harm to either party, did not produce any kind of emotional connection between victim and offender. In another conference, however, the victim and her family felt deep anger towards the offender prior to the conference and had 'made up their mind' that he was a bad person and not to be forgiven. So they did everything they could to dominate and deride him.

He [the offender] began to recount what he did and the victim kept sniping in with comments. 'That's not right. You didn't do that'... So I allowed that for a while. She jumped in and said, 'Wow, am I upset, wow!' And off she went. Once she had done that I said, 'OK, now I'm going to come back to [the offender] and then I will give you a chance to get it all off your chest.' 'Well that's not …!' And off she went onto another tryst. I mean this woman had gone past boiling point. She was now on rant. Well, I just let her go. I could see [the offender] sitting there, and his mum. The colour was draining from mum's face. And [he] was just sitting there, like, what should I do? She didn't really let him go, she was like a monkey on his back.

Neither the offender nor his mother had a chance to participate. Whenever he attempted to speak, the victim interrupted him, thus preventing the series of exchanges needed to establish a rhythm. Whether or not this woman's anger was justified (she was, after all, the victim of a serious burglary) her behaviour was contrary to restorative principles, which are based on respect for the views of all participants while they are sitting in the circle. The negative effects of the victim's behaviour on the offender and his mother were clearly observable. They both tried to speak in the beginning but, after having all their attempts overpowered, fell silent for the rest of the conference, with the offender holding back tears of frustration. The offender's mum, who was upset and crying, made a final attempt at reconciliation:

So she got up out of her seat, and she went across to the victim, she got on her knees. And I think she tried to sort of embrace her, but the victim moved away from her...there she was, on her knees, trying to say sorry...And she [the victim] wouldn't have it. She turned her body, her body posture was already like that [sitting straight up, facing slightly away from the group]. But she turned around, and totally blanked her. She gave her the whole of her side and her back.

This moment marked the 'end' of the conference, according to the facilitator. At this point it became clear to everyone, including the facilitator, that any successful or productive outcome would not take place.

Imbalance may be initiated by the victim, the offender, or the supporters, and it presents a challenge to the facilitator to restore equilibrium. Take, for instance, a conference involving an incident of road rage where a young, muscular man physically assaulted an elderly man whose driving angered him—he headbutted him and caused him to be hospitalized and in need of stitches. In this case the offender brought his girlfriend and both his parents to the conference while the victim came on his own.

They argued for about twenty minutes about who did what driving. Who was a good driver and who was a bad driver? The victim started to justify his own driving, saying he had been driving for years. And very little was said about his injury. And I think that one went quite badly wrong because they ended up with the offender's party effectively telling the victim that he ought to go and get another driving test and that he may not be suitable to drive on the road at his age.

This case was imbalanced from the start—the offender had a number of aggressive supporters while the victim did not have any. He was also unable or unwilling to discuss his injuries and the effects of the assault on him. With this imbalance, a rhythm never developed and the conference consisted mainly of the offender and his supporters doing the talking, with only occasional input from the victim when he attempted to defend himself or justify his driving. At one point, the victim told the offender, 'It's all right for you, you've got all your family here for you, and I'm on my own.' This was a 'screaming signal…to focus on how he [the victim] felt but it wasn't picked up'. Here, the combination of the unchecked aggression directed at the victim by the offender and his family, and the facilitator's failure to recognize or correct the imbalance, led to an unproductive conference.

Participants may use different strategies to restore the balance of a conference, and often in unexpected ways. In a conference where the offender appeared to be particularly manipulative and insincere as she eagerly tried to defend and justify herself, and the victim was so very upset she hardly had a chance to talk about her harm, it seemed that the conference had quickly became 'overbalanced' in the offender's favour.

Up until that time she [the victim] had been afraid, and she was crying. The offender walked across the room and offered to shake the victim's hand. She said, 'If it will make you feel better I want to shake your hand.'…But the victim said, 'I don't want your hand.' It was at that point that she started to get her life back. And she started to take control. She talked about the fact that she hadn't gone back to work. By this time [the offender] had started crying, it was beginning to have an effect on her, you can see tears in her eyes.

By refusing an insincere attempt at reconciliation, the victim restored the balance of power in the conference and both the victim and offender began to contribute equally, engaging with each other through back and forth interaction.

The Role of Supporters

As we have seen, the participation of supporters often helps to stabilize the rhythm of a conference. As Table 5.2 shows, there is a substantial difference in the number of supporters attending the different types of conference and, compared with the worst conferences, the most successful conferences had, on average, an additional two people in the circle. The best conferences also had

Table 5.2 Mean Number of Participants and Supporters by Conference Type

	Successes (n = 9)	Typical (n = 6)	Failures (n = 9)
Participants	6.44	4.17	4.67
Offender supporters	2.33	0.83	1.89
Victim supporters	2.00	1.49	0.78

more supporters on both the offenders' and victims' sides, while the worst conferences particularly lacked victim supporters.

The role of the supporters is often critical. Offender supporters can feel more empowered to challenge an offender's narrative than anyone else in the room, as in the conference discussed above where the offender's brother stood up and challenged him to speak. As well as filling vital gaps in the narrative of events, they can also provide useful details about the offender's current situation and background.

I do prefer to have at least two on each side, it takes the pressure off the victim and the perpetrator. And also it adds a little more honesty to the conference, because people try to get away with some things that are bollocks.

For example, one successful case involved an artifice burglary, where the offender knocked on a series of doors at the homes of elderly people posing as a repair man. After they invited him in to their homes, he would steal from them when they weren't looking. In this conference the victim, an elderly woman, was accompanied by her daughter. The facilitator was pleased with this. As he describes it:

The daughter was a teacher, and I thought this was great. She was an art teacher or something like that, and she had a son who was about the same age as the offender. And I said to her 'wonderful', because I explained to her, 'what this guy does is trick people'. So having someone like her...who has already had a lot of experience with people this age, and in particular boys, because she taught in an all boys school, I said you would be really useful to have. Because you will be able to tell whether this guy is telling the truth or not.

Victim supporters can help articulate the effects of an incident on a victim by providing a full account of the harm. When supporters are not present, this accounting may not take place, as in the earlier road rage conference where the offender's family acted in his defence and the victim, an elderly man living on his own, had no supporters at all. This distorted the course of events so that the victim was made to feel like he was the one who had caused harm due to his poor driving. In this case he ended up apologizing, feeling as if he had made a big fuss over nothing and was the cause of this young man being in a lot of trouble. The story told by the group was not one of a healthy, strong man seriously assaulting an elderly, defenceless driver for a minor traffic frustration. The facilitator noted that this was an instance where victim supporters could have been particularly helpful in bringing some balance to the conference.

While supporters are important, they are likely to be most effective when they have a significant relationship with the victim or offender. If supporters are unavailable (particularly for the offender), a facilitator may bring in a 'professional supporter' such as a social worker, drug counsellor, or chaplain and while they may be important players in a conference, some facilitators find their presence to be awkward and contrived and even describe them as 'wastes of space'. They further argue that while a professional supporter may not harm the conference, they do not add to its emotional intensity. For instance, in a conference relating to an employee theft from a chain retail store, company headquarters decided to send a personnel manager along to act as a corporate representative. While other participants in the conference had close personal connections with the offender and the event (they were her co-workers and former friends who had also been suspected of the theft), the company representative knew no one personally and had little knowledge of the theft apart from what she had read in the report. As a result, the facilitator found her to be 'the least helpful'.

She seemed to really come from the company's perspective. I don't think that added to it because the whole conference revolves around how everybody felt. They listened to her politely, and then moved on to something else. And she didn't even know anybody in the room.

Her participation was one negative aspect in an otherwise very successful conference.

Turning Points

A final common element of a successful conference is the 'turning points'. These are specific moments, or a series of moments, where rhythm and entrainment coalesce and disruptions cease. According to facilitators, turning points act as emotional epiphanies that bring people together. It is where the ritual outcomes of a conference, such as displays of solidarity between offenders and victims, become apparent. Conferences that lack turning points may be described as 'flat'. For example, when prompted to explain what went wrong with a conference identified as 'unsuccessful', one facilitator responded that, '[i]t just wasn't that good ultimately. It didn't have the impact. It didn't have the moment that you talk about, like a cathartic moment...where everybody starts to get on. That just didn't happen at all.'

Turning points can be dramatic and confronting. Take the case described earlier where the victim's wife suffered an attack of stress-related eczema. The conference started off quite badly when she refused to shake hands with the offender; stared at him with open hostility, and interrupted both the offender and her husband with comments that were 'full of anger'. There was a change, however, when it came to her turn to speak uninterrupted, 'All at once the anger and disdain that had been present in all my conversations with her prior to the conference had subsided to constructive words.' She clearly and emotionally described the effect the robbery had on her and her family.

And she said, 'Before I met you, I wanted to kill you.' And she slammed her fist into her hand. The offender moved back. She slowly and in order told of all the effects. The effects on her son, her family, her work, her eczema. I don't think he expected such an outpouring, or for it to be so descriptive. She went into it. A day or two after she found out about the crime and that her husband had been to the hospital...her eczema flared so much in the night that she woke up and some of her clothing was stuck to her body, where the eczema had seeped. So she had to get into the bath, and peel her pyjamas off. Shocking.

As she described everything in a calm, clear voice the facilitator observed a change in the offender, who he had described as 'slightly cynical' before going into the conference. According to the facilitator, you could see her story 'sink into him'. Before that moment, however, he did not 'embrace the gravity of what he was going to do [in the conference]. And I prefer people like that. Because they walk in cynical, thinking, it's something to do. And they get thumped with all this hurt and anger, and I think it was wonderful. I think it was a fantastic thing.'

Turning points can also build over time. In the earlier example of balance being restored, when the victim sensed the offender's insincerity and rebuffed her attempt at a handshake it marked the beginning of a series of turning points including one where the offender's aunt began to cry so hard she was unable to speak. 'And it was at that point that [the offender] began to realize what she had done. Because she obviously had a great deal of regard for her aunt and to see her aunt crying as a result of her actions, that did it for her.' After that, the conference took on a completely different tone with most of the participants either crying or sniffling. Then the victim called the offender back across the circle, grasped her hands and began to pray for her.

And it was at that point where there were no dry eyes in the conference. I think everybody, even the observers, started crying. In fact I think the observer even thought that it was staged. It was so emotional and so powerful. She actually prayed for her. And after the conference the victim walked out with her head held high.

This conference took a few separate encounters to turn. First, the victim's refusal of an initial handshake woke the offender up to her harm. Then, the emotional breakdown of the offender's aunt drove it home. Next, the victim initiated physical contact and, by then, the emotional power of the moment was so strong that it even affected the observers sitting outside the conference circle. Such turning points lead to one of the main ritual outcomes, that is, the expression of solidarity of the group.

There is some evidence to suggest that gender may play a significant role when there is a turning point in restorative justice conferences because, as in many interactions, women contribute to the emotional work involved in bringing the group together and allowing collective feeling to emerge (Hochschild, 1983). Similarly, the data from these conferences shows that the best conferences, on average, have much higher female-to-male ratios than the worst (see Table 5.3). As one facilitator recalled when thinking back to all his best conferences, it was always a woman—usually an offender or victim supporter—who sparked a turning point. Other facilitators supported this impression. In every successful case reviewed, a turning point was precipitated by a woman exhibiting a range of emotions including tears of anger, disappointment, and frustration.

Conferences [without women] aren't as emotional. Men tend to hide their feelings, they're not very good at explaining their feelings even if they want

Table 5.3 Gender Participants by Conference Type

	Successes (n = 9)	Typical (n = 6)	Failures (n = 9)
Mean number of women	3.78	2.00	1.67
Mean number of men	2.67	2.17	2.89
Ratio of women to men	1.41	0.92	0.58

to. It is more of a macho thing. So yes, it makes quite a difference if you have a woman. Women are more open, I think they lay their cards on the table a lot more, where men tend to keep their cards close to their chest, don't want to expose weaknesses. Whereas it is more natural for women to say 'These are my weaknesses, you hit me here, you pushed that pressure point there, which caused this emotional reaction.' Men often don't even know what causes their emotions, or are too proud to say it.

Perhaps men often rely on women to bring about the emotional release that allows them to let down their guards and engage fully in the proceedings of restorative justice conferences. Maybe women are more likely to turn a conference into a successful ritual. This is an area that needs further attention.

Conclusion

Facilitators work hard to prepare participants for powerful rituals. There is a complicated period of setting up both the physical and emotional elements of the conference. In this preparatory stage, facilitators must solve a range of operational problems, such as arranging a suitable time, date, and location; ensuring all participants are there; and, often, negotiating with prisons. They are also engaged in a kind of emotional labour, building trust and rapport with each participant; finding suitable supporters and evaluating the role each person will play; and carefully building up the emotional intensity with each participant so that they will be ready to perform on the day.

If this preparatory work runs according to plan, the elements of a successful interaction ritual can appear during the conference. Nervous and disjointed talk will smooth into a rhythm over time, as participants ease into turn-taking. Imbalance and disempowerment will be minimized, often through the careful use of supporters. A specific dramatic moment (or series of them) acts as a turning point, providing a focus of attention for all participants and bringing them all together in a feeling of ritual group intensity. By contrast, in failed rituals there is no rhythm; participants are uncomfortable the entire time; one party dominates the other; and there is no dramatic turning point. There is a distinct lack of transformation for those attending, who may also see such encounters as having been a waste of time.

When the elements of successful rituals are in place, the positive outcomes of such encounters emerge. These include group level emotions of solidarity, shared morality, and emotional energy. The way these concepts are constructed in restorative justice conferences will be explored in Chapter Six.

6

Short-Term Outcomes in Restorative Justice

Chapter Five focused on the strategies facilitators use in the lead-up to and during a restorative justice conference to both prepare participants and develop the rhythm and balance which characterize a successful ritual. In interviews with facilitators about their most and least successful conferences, they revealed the techniques they proactively use to set up the ritual. In this chapter I explore ways to observe and measure ritual outcomes of successful restorative justice conferences. First, I draw on the qualitative situational analyses conducted through in-depth interviews with police facilitators about their best, worst, and typical conferences, which comprise a total pool of twenty-four conferences. Similar to Chapter Five, I find examinations of failed rituals to be particularly instructive. Using the themes developed in the qualitative research, the second half of the chapter introduces the Reintegrative Shaming Experiments ('RISE') study from Canberra, Australia (Sherman et al, 1998; Sherman, Strang, and Woods, 2000). I analyse systematic observations of 124 conferences to develop a statistical model of interaction rituals in restorative justice conferences.

Ritual Outcomes

Insights from sociology and anthropology suggest that positive outcomes of successful rituals include solidarity, the development of symbols representing shared morality, and a short-term burst of emotional energy (Durkheim, 1912; Collins, 2004). These are immediate, in-the-moment positive outcomes.

Solidarity

Solidarity in a restorative justice conference manifests in physical contact between and among parties, for example, between victim and offender, or between their supporters. It includes shaking hands, touching, hugging, and eye contact. In their training facilitators expressed scepticism when they were told that conferences were often powerful events in which people may cry and even hug. They could not believe an offender and victim would ever voluntarily touch one another, let alone hug. However, they later reported that, contrary to expectations, hugging was a relatively common event at conferences and, when asked to pinpoint the best part of a conference, often related an instance in which participants embraced. Of the 'successful conferences' described by facilitators in the study, all nine contained a spontaneous instance of physical contact between the victim's and offender's sides (see Table 6.1). For instance, one facilitator recalled this happening in a conference that he described as 'the best thing I have ever done'.

R: (Victim's) mum was now crying. [The offender's] mum then comes out of her seat, she steps forward and kneels down in front of her (victim's mum) and starts hugging her. Gorgeous…So I went to get some tea, and they got up and they all just started hugging. It was a mass hug-a-thon. All hugging.

I: Who initiated it?

R: I just couldn't work it out. Because it all seemed to happen instantaneously.

In the typical and failed conferences, however, touching occurred in only four of the former and two of the latter, and these were more likely to be in the form of formal handshakes that were initiated by the facilitator at the beginning or end of a conference.

Sustained eye contact also indicates solidarity and facilitators observed such eye contact in eight out of nine successful conferences.

Table 6.1 Ritual Outcomes by Conference Type

	Successful (n = 9)	Typical (n = 6)	Failures (n = 9)
Touching	9 (100%)	4 (67%)	2 (22%)
Eye contact	8 (89)	6 (100)	4 (44)
Apology made	8 (89)	6 (100)	7 (78)
Apology accepted	8 (89)	6 (100)	4 (44)
Crying	8 (89)	3 (50)	4 (44)
Smiling	7 (78)	5 (83)	1 (11)
Laughing	5 (56)	0 (0)	0 (0)

For example, in a successful conference it was noted that participants' 'eyes were pointing in [each others'] direction. He was nodding and you would get a reply. They were intensely engaged with each other.' In unsuccessful conferences, however, participants maintained eye contact in only four out of nine conferences. As one facilitator recounted when discussing a failed conference, the victims were either looking down or 'off centre, staring into space' the whole time. They avoided direct eye contact with both the offender and his supporters throughout the conference.

Typically, conference participants are hesitant to look at each other and tend to focus their gaze on the facilitator. To discourage this, facilitators use the 'click and drag' technique where they lock eyes with a victim, for example, and then 'drag' their eyes to the offender's. They generally use the technique at the beginning of a conference when people are reluctant to engage with each other. If successful, this leads to the offender and victim looking directly at each other. As one facilitator noted, 'People automatically look at you, so I would use the click and drag to get eyes off me and onto each other.'

Symbols of relationship

Potential symbols of the relationship that develops between participants in a conference include the outcome agreement, and the exchange of apology and forgiveness between the victim and the offender. Retzinger and Scheff have noted that symbolic reparation is the vital element in conferences and point to a 'core sequence' of the expression of remorse followed by forgiveness as the strongest symbol of a repaired bond (Retzinger and Scheff, 1996). Collins adds that symbolic representations are important because they act as an ongoing reminder of the positive emotions experienced (Collins, 2004). Can restorative justice conferences provide such symbols?

One symbol is perhaps embodied in the outcome agreement that participants formulate and sign. In the final stage of a conference, the participants shift their focus from the incident and its aftermath to a forward-thinking collaborative deliberation on how the offender can 'repair the harm' to the victim and the larger community. This can include a symbolic gesture, such as writing a letter of apology to the victim, or it can involve instrumental tasks such as making financial reparations, agreeing to see a therapist, or attending drug rehabilitation. The items that go into an outcome agreement arise out of the group's discussion and are unique to the group. Once agreement is reached, it is signed by all the participants and individual copies are given to everyone to take home.

In theory, the outcome agreement, or elements of it, symbolizes the successful interaction and highlights a new standard of morality shared by the participants. In practice, however, it may be regarded as less important than the emotional interaction, communication, and shared understanding that has occurred during an actual successful conference. For example, a facilitator tells me, 'I don't think the outcome agreement was the important thing. The important thing here was that these people got that huge shared understanding of what had gone on.' As the facilitator suggests, the emotional breakthrough that can happen in a conference may not always be represented on a piece of paper that everybody signs. A truly heartfelt and meaningful apology that significantly impacted the victim may not appear heartfelt or meaningful when written into an outcome agreement.

By the time it comes to the part of the conference where everyone is asked to devise and sign the outcome agreement, the peak emotional focus of the conference may have come and gone. When this happens, as it often does in a successful conference, the outcome agreement may no longer represent an appropriate symbol of the interaction and facilitators reported that they sometimes found it a struggle to think of things to add to the outcome agreement that would impress a judge because it did not, and could not, really reflect what actually took place. For this reason, the facilitators did not always see much value in the outcome agreement in their best conferences. In describing a favourite conference, a facilitator explains, 'I think this was a conference where the outcome agreement was very much secondary. I think that the victim was able to move on, having seen [the] defendant and realizing that she was not a headless monster.'

The exchange of apology and forgiveness between the offender and victim is another potential symbol of a conference, echoing the 'core sequence' described by Retzinger and Scheff (1996). Offenders apologize in almost every case and a lot of formal attention is paid to this because they are usually recorded in the outcome agreement. Such exchanges are implicitly written into the script as when participants describe how they have been affected, the facilitator then looks to the offender to ask if there is anything they want to say. An apology at this point is almost guaranteed. In both the best and worst conferences, facilitators reported an apology from the offender.

I: Do you think that verbal apologies are important parts of a conference?

R: That's a good question. Sometimes they are and sometimes they can be a very cynical apology or insincere apology; sometimes, I think the deeds far outweigh an apology. If someone apologized that's all well and good, they are stretching their hand out by saying I am really sorry, I honestly and genuinely am sorry for what I did to you, then excellent. But sometimes the offenders are trying to say sorry, and victims were going yeah right that is a bunch of bollocks, crap. It's very easy to apologize. I can apologize to you for anything in this room, it's so easy to do.

It seems that apologies need to be 'genuine' in order to be meaningful. While this may be difficult to measure in a rigorous sense, one way of assessing it is by noting whether the apology was combined with some expression of forgiveness or acceptance. In the successful conferences, seven out of nine apologies were accepted by the victims whereas in less than half of the worst conferences were apologies accepted (see Table 6.2). In the latter, however, the apologies were interpreted by the victims as insincere.

This suggests that while the exchange of apology and forgiveness may be a powerful symbol, formalizing it into the script of the conference will lessen some of its strength. Facilitators walk a fine line between encouraging the spontaneous expression of emotions while keeping it fresh and not routinized. Not surprisingly, facilitators have expressed to me that the best way to achieve this is by ensuring participants are well prepared. This makes sense. If the right ingredients are there for a good interaction ritual then there will be a spontaneous creation of symbols to represent the shared bond.

Emotional energy

Emotional energy stems from group solidarity and shared morality and is the positive charge that participants take from the group and into future interactions. It is an important outcome of a successful interaction ritual and has short- and long-term effects.

High emotional energy is a long-term feeling of confidence and initiative towards social goals; low emotional energy is a feeling of depression and withdrawal from those goals. Emotional energy provides the possibility for long-term effects and keeps the interaction from being fleeting. It is also perhaps the most difficult outcome to measure as it is both a short- and long-term outcome. Its long-term consequence in a successful interaction ritual is that its effects can stay with a participant well after the event.

A person's body language is easily observable in a restorative justice conference and Collins (2004: 134) suggests that the immediate emotional energy of a participant in a successful interaction ritual can be measured by examining posture and demeanour. One example from Chapter Five was where the facilitator described an elderly victim who was hunched over, with her head down, 'trying to make herself look small'. By the end of the conference, they observed, 'The victim looked different. The victim actually looked taller. Everything about her. It was almost like some big thing had happened, and she just looked better, standing up straighter, her head was higher.' In another example, the wife of a victim remarked after the conference that she felt 'looser'. In fact, in a burst of emotional energy after the conference, the victim and his wife were able to do something he had not been able to do since the attack, and that was to visit the scene of the crime 'because he felt like he needed to go back. He felt like he had exorcized a few ghosts in the meeting and he wanted to go back to where the crime was committed.' The interaction with the offender had charged him up enough to motivate an action that had previously frightened him.

The posture of the offender is also a marker of emotional energy in a successful conference as when facilitators observed differences in the offender's posture between the beginning and end of the conference: 'I think he was nervous and very sort of, nervous, head down, body language, hunched over. But as the conference went on, and he felt less threatened, he felt more relaxed to open up and carry his body a little bit more.'

While erect posture is common in a successful conference, the opposite is true in a negative one. In a conference marked by imbalance and a lack of rhythm, in which the victim disbelieved everything the offender said and constantly challenged him to tell the truth, the facilitator observed, 'I remember he [the offender] was looking down. And then I think that once the victim challenged him, then he sat with his legs crossed, sort of disengaged.' Thereafter, the offender withdrew from the conversation and remained uninvolved and downcast for the rest of the time.

Tea and biscuits and the return to normalcy

There is a final, informal stage of the conference where participants break for tea or coffee and sign the outcome agreement. While not an official part of restorative justice, many facilitators see it as providing an opportunity for participants to relax and engage in 'normal talk'—informal discussion about work, football, the neighbourhood, or anything else that happens to come up. This allows offenders, victims, and their supporters to engage with one another as ordinary people and helps to draw them back into the real world. It can also be the place for acts of symbolic reparation, as in the case study from Chapter Four when the victim's husband offers a biscuit to the offender's infant son.

Schechner (1981), in his analysis of theatre as ritual, identifies a need for a cooling down period after a climax. He argues that in contemporary western theatre, too much emphasis is placed on preparation, rehearsal, and warm up, with little attention paid to closures. He points to dramatic practices in Bali, where performers engage in rituals for cooling down, such as sprinkling themselves with holy water, inhaling incense, and massage. These rituals transport you back to an everyday state, and mark the ritual that came before it as a sacred or special event.

In a successful conference, the elevated experience may be full of collective effervescence but participants need to come back down and take roles other than those of offender, victim, or supporter. In this stage they are just ordinary people drinking tea together. According to one facilitator, '[I]t is the official end that underlines the event nature of the conference…a bit like a celebration.' Drinking tea and talking informally allows the intensity levels to drop and, in an interesting twist, on a few occasions participants have even decided to pray together at this time—with the shared prayer helping to shift the group back to normalcy.

Empirical Model of Interaction Ritual in Restorative Justice

Having explored the elements of interaction ritual in the preparatory and beginning stages of the conference, and the short-term ritual outcomes, the next step will be to use some of the key concepts identified in the qualitative research to quantitatively test for the elements of interaction ritual in systematic observations of restorative justice conferences.

Qualitative interviews and an in-depth examination of a video recording of a conference were useful tools for exploring the elements of interaction ritual in restorative justice. Such a qualitative approach allows for a deeper exploration of the dynamics and processes at work in restorative justice. On the other hand, quantitative analysis can identify patterns and underlying structures that contribute to success or failure. By combining the two approaches, qualitative and quantitative, the aim is to develop an empirical model of interaction ritual in restorative justice.

Although it may be argued that the translation of these concepts and constructs into quantitative variables is flawed because the reductive nature of survey items would fail to capture the situational and dynamic elements of a conference as it unfolds, we do the best with what we have. And what we have is an exciting and ground-breaking source of data drawn from the RISE study—the largest, longest running study of restorative justice ever conducted (Sherman and Strang, 2007). The RISE study has informed theory, practice, and policy in restorative justice since its inception in the mid-1990s and continues to be a landmark piece of research. (For a full description of the study, see Chapter Three.)

Specifically, this analysis used the systematic observations of restorative justice conferences in the Juvenile Violent Crime ('JVC') experiment and the Juvenile Personal Property ('JPP') experiment. The JVC experiment involved violent offences (assaults and robberies) committed by people under 30 years old, and the JPP experiment included property crimes such as burglaries, thefts, and criminal damage. The mean age of offenders was 18.02 years for the JVC conferences and 15.6 years for the JPP conferences. See Table 6.2 for further descriptive statistics of the two samples.

In most conferences a trained observer from the research team used a detailed observation guide, the Global Observational Ratings Instrument, to record what happened. Observers took notes during the conference and then immediately afterwards completed the instrument. The Global Observational Ratings Instrument consisted of a number of eight-point items measuring a range of elements of the conference and documenting such things as shame, remorse, and forgiveness. The items in the observation instrument encompassed a range of important behaviours such as how the offender acted towards the victim(s), how the supporter(s) and victim(s) treated the offender, and changes in demeanour and emotional states. Because it enabled researchers to measure concepts that are central to understanding emotional dynamics in conferences, many of the items could also be used to explore and measure interaction ritual.

Table 6.2 Sample Characteristics

	No.	%
Experiment		
Property (JPP)	85	63.43
Violence (JVC)	49	36.57
Total	*134*	*100.0*
Offence		
Arson	6	4.5
Assault	33	24.6
Burglary	13	9.7
Criminal damage	15	11.2
Fraud	2	1.5
Robbery	6	4.5
Theft	54	40.3
Weapon	2	1.5
Missing	3	2.2
Total	*134*	*100.0*
Mean Age	16.5	
Gender		
Male	113	84.3
Female	21	15.7
Total	*134*	*100.0*
Race		
Non-indigenous	98	73.1
Indigenous	13	9.7
Missing	23	17.2
Total	*134*	*100.0*

The large-scale nature of RISE required numerous observers over time so it was necessary to carry out reliability tests to test for a high degree of inter-rater reliability (Harris and Burton, 1998). At the same time, because the instrument was initially developed to focus on the action, behaviour, and treatment of the offender, the observations were skewed towards the offender and were not necessarily representative of the emotional atmosphere of the situation as a whole. I have addressed this in the analysis however, by focusing on items that include group dynamics, such as how many interruptions took place, whether there was an exchange of apology and forgiveness, or if anyone shook hands or touched. Appendix Four details the observation items used.

Systematic observation is a highly accurate way to measure emotions and interactional dynamics compared with interviews and surveys which, because they are conducted after the emotional event, may not be reliable measures of subjects' feelings and behaviour. A decay in delicate feelings and memories may have set in by then and participants may not remember exactly what they were feeling at the time. A trained observer using an observation instrument, however, is able to document emotional dynamics and behaviours as they occur with a high degree of accuracy. These can then be mined as a rich source of data to inform a model of interaction ritual in restorative justice conferences.

The first step was to decide which items could be used to measure the elements of interaction ritual. To accomplish this, I employed a combination of exploratory and confirmatory factor analyses which are useful statistical methods for identifying the underlying structure of sets of variables. Exploratory factor analysis is useful when you have a large number of items (such as in the RISE observation instrument) and you want to determine which items are most correlated with each other and can, therefore, be grouped into distinct 'factors'. Confirmatory factor analysis is a slightly more sophisticated technique, useful for when you want to fit a number of items to specific factors. In this case, we have a theory about the ingredients and outcomes of an interaction ritual that we want to test, and we want to see if we can make a factor to represent each element of the theory. For example, if we take a major outcome of an interaction ritual—the externalization of solidarity—we can use confirmatory factor analysis to identify which items on the observation instrument can act, when taken together, as some kind of reliable measure of 'solidarity'. As seen earlier in this chapter, we already have some inkling of what kinds of measures may be used, such as touching, making eye contact, laughing, or hugging. Confirmatory factor analysis takes these and other such measures and is able to fit them into a statistical model to create reliable measures for solidarity.

The data used to develop interaction ritual ingredients and outcomes, as laid out by Collins (2004) and explored in Chapters Four and Five, involve clear components and dimensions. In addition, the qualitative data collected on conferencing suggest that specific factors are important to the success of a conference. Such a strong theoretical and empirical background makes confirmatory factor analysis an appropriate and useful method for this data.

In this way, we are able to test different factor models to see which best fits the available data while at the same time maintaining the structure of interaction ritual theory.

The Structure of a Ritual

The factor analysis identified six distinct factors to represent the ingredients and outcomes of an interaction ritual (see Table 6.3),[1] with factors one to three representing ritual ingredients, and factors four to six representing ritual outcomes.

Table 6.3 Interaction Ritual Ingredients and Outcomes

	No.	Mean	Standard Deviation
Factor 1—Balance ($\alpha = 0.76$)			
How much was offender dominated?	124	5.48	2.14
How much did offender contribute to the conference?	117	3.62	1.47
Percentage of time offender talking	117	2.71	0.74
How much did the offender contribute to the conference outcome?	124	3.27	1.82
Factor 2—Stigmatization ($\alpha = 0.76$)			
Stigmatizing shaming expressed	124	2.02	1.46
Offender treated as a criminal	124	1.57	1.04
Stigmatizing names used to describe offender	124	1.40	0.88
Disapproval of the offender as a person expressed	124	2.40	1.60

[1] The exploratory factor analysis initially identified five factors using various criteria including the scree plot, eigenvalue, and general comprehensibility, which account for 58.1% of the variance. However, certain items that were relevant to interaction ritual theory, such as whether or not there was touching, hugging, or crying, did not load on these five factors. I included them when fitting the model during confirmatory factor analysis because they were relevant to the theory. The confirmatory factor analysis was conducted using the structural equation modelling software AMOS. Initially, a one factor model was tested which included all the potential items from the observations. As hypothesized, this proved a poor fit for the data, indicating that a multidimensional model would be more appropriate. Following that, two, three, four, five, six, and seven factor models were tested. Each additional factor improved the model fit, using the CFI, AIC, BCC, and RMSEA scores as goodness-of-fit criteria, with an emphasis on a parsimonious model. A sic factor model provided the best fit (chi square = 563, AIC = 743.71, BCC = 787.45, RMSEA = 0.094, CFI = 0.820). The fit statistics suggest there is

Table 6.3 Continued

	No.	Mean	Standard Deviation
Factor 3—Defiance (α = 0.55)			
Offender claimed actions were accidental	124	2.37	2.19
Offender held others responsible	123	2.39	1.99
Offender had defiant attitude	124	2.13	1.76
Factor 4—Reintegration (α = 0.91)			
Offender was given support during the conference	124	5.47	1.60
Conference was reintegrative for the offender	124	4.97	2.02
Approval of the offender as a person was expressed	124	4.27	1.88
Offender was treated by their supporters as one they love	124	5.44	1.81
Factor 5—Solidarity (α = 0.73)			
Any touching? (% yes)	124	16.10	
Did the offender apologize? (% yes)	124	83.90	
Was the offender forgiven for his actions?	122	4.11	2.11
How much forgiveness was expressed?	121	2.91	2.03
Offender was sorry or remorseful	124	5.37	2.05
Factor 6—Emotional Energy[1] (α = 0.90)			
Offender appeared sullen (reverse coded)	115	6.21	2.05
Offender retreated or avoided attention of others	124	5.48	2.18
Offender's speech affected by irregularities and pauses	124	6.13	2.07
Offender uncomfortable	124	4.38	2.04
Offender engaged in hiding behaviour	124	5.48	2.30

[1]these items were all reverse coded

Ritual ingredients

Factor one items represent conversational balance which is consistent with the qualitative data explored in Chapter Five. They include measures of how much the offender was dominated, how much they contributed to the conference as a whole, the percentage

room for improvement in this model such as better measures to capture the ritual ingredients and outcomes. One must acknowledge that this data was not originally collected with a mind to test interaction ritual theory. This is the best approximation with the available data. Future research will include further systematic observations of restorative justice with an explicit focus on the development of interaction ritual.

of time the offender spoke, and how much they contributed to the conference outcome ($\alpha = 0.763$). Factors two and three are both indicators of the general rhythm and flow of the interaction. Factor two items represent stigmatization including how much stigmatizing shame was expressed, how much disapproval of the offender as a person was expressed, how often stigmatizing names and labels were used to describe the offender, and how much the offender was treated like a criminal. These stigmatizing items may indicate the general power and status games played during the interaction ($\alpha = 0.763$). Factor three represented defiant behaviour on the part of the offender including the extent to which the offender claimed their actions were accidental, how much they held others responsible for their actions, and overall defiant behaviour ($\alpha = 0.548$). This type of behaviour indicates where the offender may have caused disruptions in the flow of the interaction.

Stigmatization and defiance items, taken together, can be seen as potential disrupters to the rhythmic flow of conversation. A conference marked by stigmatizing behaviour towards the offender or acts of defiance can be seen as a conference where the back and forth, rhythmic entrainment of conversation is never allowed to develop fully.

Balance, stigmatization, and defiance are indicators of how the conversation was progressing and whether rhythmic entrainment was developing. Their failure to correlate highly with each other, as shown in Table 6.4, seems also to confirm that they are distinct factors. When taken together, however, they can be seen to contribute to the overall emotional tone in a conference. Their presence confirms that we can distinguish the ingredients of an interaction ritual.

The rhythm factors (stigmatization and defiance) describe participants' predisposition towards one another as well as how

Table 6.4 Factor Correlations

Ritual Factors	1	2	3	4	5	6
1 Balance	1					
2 Stigmatization	−0.18**	1				
3 Defiance	−0.06	0.03	1			
4 Reintegration	0.40**	−0.38**	−0.39**	1		
5 Solidarity	0.28*	−0.30**	−0.39**	0.70**	1	
6 Emotional Energy	0.43**	−0.28**	0.05	0.12	0.17	1

*p <.05; **p<.01

they treated each other during the conference. They also indicate whether an offender was acting defiantly, not taking responsibility for their actions, behaving as though they were unhappy to be there, and refusing to willingly engage (either conversationally or emotionally) with either the victim's or their own supporters.

On the victim's (and their supporters') side, acts of stigmatization can work to draw clear status boundaries between themselves and the offender and this lack of inclusiveness inhibits the back and forth emotional entrainment required for a successful interaction. An example of this can be found in the conference where the victims rearranged the chairs to avoid sitting anywhere near the offender. In this case, the victim had made up her mind in advance about what kind of person the offender was and, as she told the facilitator, she was unwilling to take into account anything he said. In the conference, her language and actions towards the offender conveyed stigmatization: 'I know what kind of person you are, you're scum, and that's all you will ever be.' According to the facilitator, such statements, which continued to be made throughout the conference, created a barrier to the development of rhythm.

Also drawing from the qualitative evidence, we saw how acts of defiance contribute to disruptions in the rhythm, such as in the road rage case where a young offender had assaulted an elderly man because he was frustrated with the way he was driving. In that conference, the offender blamed and abused the victim rather than take responsibility for his own violent actions. The victim ended up apologizing to the offender for being a bad driver and suggested that he deserved the assault! In this conference, the offender and his supporters ganged up on the victim, who was never able to discuss how he had been affected, physically and emotionally, by the assault. There was no emotional entrainment between the participants and no conversational rhythm, and the conference was an example of how defiant behaviour on the part of the offender can lead to a lack of rhythm developing.

Ritual outcomes

Factor four (reintegration ($\alpha = 0.912$)) contains items that indicate the amount of support, approval, and love given to the offender. It should be noted, however, that the wording of the items makes it difficult to distinguish whether the reintegration is between offender and victim or offender and supporters, so these items may only be a measure of reintegration between the offender and their supporters. The items are similar to those used to represent reintegration by Ahmed et al (2001) and Tyler et al (2007). While these studies also use the RISE data, they do not employ such a strict statistical model as confirmatory factor analysis. It is testament to the intuitive accuracy of the method that the results were so comparable.

Factor five (group solidarity) consisted of items that measure if the offender apologized, their level of remorse, how much forgiveness was implicitly and explicitly expressed, and whether there was any touching (handshakes, hugs, pats on the back) ($\alpha = 0.725$). In this sense, solidarity indicated acts and behaviour that unite people, such as the exchange of apology and forgiveness as well as physical manifestations like touching, which were apparent in the qualitative analysis.

Solidarity is a measure of group togetherness and reintegration is an indicator of positive emotions directed towards an offender. As measures, they are statistically, and meaningfully, distinct from each other. Solidarity measures are externalizations of social bonding between offender and victim; barriers are crossed and people meet each other on the same level. Reintegration, on the other hand, measures particular emotions and actions directed towards the offender such as support, approval, and love—with the focus on the relationship between the offender and their supporters rather than the offender and victim.

As suggested by Ahmed et al (2001), reintegration may share a common message with procedural fairness (Tyler, 1990), with the emphasis on respect for the offender. I argue that rhythmic, fair, and balanced interactions lead to procedurally just and reintegrative outcomes. Other research also shows an association between procedural fairness and pride (Tyler, Degoey, and Smith, 1996). While we cannot measure pride with this data, the link between the two suggests that acts of reintegration may also be associated with emotional energy.

Factor six (emotional energy) measures how much the offender retreated from and avoided attention, how much speech was affected by irregularities and pauses, how much the offender engaged in hiding behaviour, and how uncomfortable and how sullen they were ($\alpha = 0.897$). Rather than rely on the self-reporting of emotions (which is often unreliable), this factor emphasizes observed changes in an individual's behaviour and demeanour that indicate emotion.

While these items have been used to measure shame in the past, I reinterpret them here as examples of a person's generalized emotional state or emotional energy. These items are direct observations of demeanour and facial expression. This is consistent with the analysis of the video in Chapter Four, and the manifestations of emotional energy explored earlier in this chapter, such as when the facilitator described a victim as 'growing taller'. Such measures, however, are only short-term indicators of emotional energy and should not be confused with a long-term emotional state. We can interpret these items as suggesting the emotional energy level of the offender at the time of the conference.

Factors four to six will be used as measures of conference outcomes, with high scores when positive emotions are produced and low scores when negative emotions are indicated. They are indicators of whether the conference is a successful ritual.

Interaction Ritual Model

Previous chapters explored the dimensions of interaction ritual in restorative justice. They also showed that one can model and measure conversational and interactional dynamics in face-to-face meetings— such as balance, acts of defiance, and stigmatization—as well as the elements of a successful conference including solidarity, emotional energy, and group reintegration. This section uses these measures to test whether the interaction ritual does in fact influence the interaction ritual outcomes.

The independent variables that represent the key interaction ritual ingredients are balance, stigmatization, and defiance. The dependent variables are solidarity, reintegration, and emotional energy. The current analysis will use a combination of bivariate and multivariate models to explore the relationship between ritual ingredients and ritual outcomes.

For bivariate analyses, the interaction ritual variables were transformed into dichotomous variables for the sake of simplicity—with values equal to or less than the mean in the 'low' category, and values above the mean in the 'high' category. For instance, values of 3.75 and below were measured as low-balance cases, and values over 3.75 were conferences with a high level of conversational balance between victim and offender. In the multivariate analysis, however, these variables were measured as the continuous constructs produced through confirmatory factor analysis.

The models also control for sex, race, and age. As Table 6.2 shows, the majority of the conferences were with white, male offenders. Recent studies suggest that the effects of restorative justice on recidivism may vary by race (Sherman, Strang, and Woods, 2004). In the personal violence conferences in RISE, indigenous offenders were found to reoffend at higher rates compared to a randomized non-restorative justice control group. The non-indigenous offenders, however, showed significantly less reoffending than the control group. This raises a number of questions about the dynamics of the conference and the role of race. For instance, are conferences with indigenous offenders and white police facilitators less likely to produce positive rituals? Such a hypothesis can be tested with this method.

I hypothesize that conferences with higher levels of balance and lower levels of defiance and stigmatization will result in higher levels of all interaction ritual outcomes—solidarity, emotional energy, and reintegration. A theory of interaction ritual would further suggest that individual level variables such as gender, race, and age are not as important as the situational variables that make up the interaction. Figure 6.1 illustrates the hypothesized model.

Stigmatization and balance variables can be taken together to represent the rhythm of a conference. Interaction ritual theory, as well as the qualitative findings, suggests that the development of a rhythmic entrainment is key to producing solidarity and other positive outcomes of a ritual. In cases where an offender is treated in a stigmatizing manner, or acts defiantly in a conference, rhythmic entrainment would not have a chance to develop. There would be no back and forth and the rules of turn-taking in conversation would not be followed. To test this, I examined both the main effects and the interaction of defiance and stigmatization to see if it was possible to measure rhythm. I also examined the interactions between

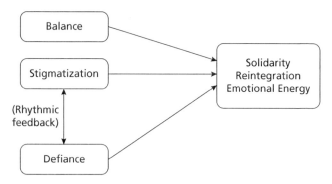

Figure 6.1 Hypothesized Model of Interaction Ritual

the control variables (race, age, and gender) and the interaction ritual ingredients to look for relationships between them.

To test these hypotheses regarding the effects of individual and ritual characteristics on ritual outcomes, I begin by examining bivariate relationships. I then use a multistep ordinary least squared regression to test the relative effects of interaction ritual ingredients and control variables on three different outcomes of an interaction ritual: solidarity, reintegration, and emotional energy. To provide a common metric for comparison, the standardized regression coefficients are reported in all the results.

Bivariate results

Bivariate associations shown in Table 6.5 suggest that conferences that were less balanced were marked by significantly lower group solidarity, displays of emotional energy, and instances of reintegration. Conversely, conferences where there was a high degree of stigmatization towards the offender tended to be characterized by lower levels of solidarity, emotional energy, and reintegration. Finally, conferences with high levels of defiant behaviour were

Table 6.5 Bivariate Relationships Among Interaction Ritual Variables

Ritual Ingredients	Ritual Outcomes		
	Solidarity	Emotional Energy	Reintegration
Balance			
Low	2.50	4.89	4.49
High	3.17	6.14	4.49
Difference	−0.67**	−1.26**	−1.11**
Stigmatization			
Low	3.05	5.74	5.35
High	2.40	5.05	4.42
Difference	0.65**	0.69*	0.94**
Defiance			
Low	3.13	5.51	5.49
High	2.42	5.50	4.40
Difference	0.71**	0.01	1.09**

*p <.05; **p<.01, two tailed t-tests

significantly associated with lower levels of both solidarity and reintegration, but defiant behaviour had no effect on emotional energy. This finding makes intuitive sense. In general, high levels of emotional energy were an indication of a successful conference, while acts of defiance on the part of the offender were hypothesized to lead to less successful outcomes. We saw earlier that emotional energy is measured by reverse codes of an offender's posture, verbal, and non-verbal actions such as stuttering, slouching, and downcast eyes. A defiant offender may actually display physical externalizations of emotional energy as a part of their defiant attitude. The results actually indicate that emotional energy levels are almost identical for low and high defiance conferences, which suggests that the relationship between defiance and emotional energy is not meaningful.

The gender and race variables were also examined in the context of interaction ritual and the bivariate results are presented in Table 6.6. There is little difference in the components of interaction ritual for males and females. The only significant finding was that female offenders are more likely to have a balanced conference than male offenders. This was especially interesting in the light of a

Table 6.6 **Bivariate Relationship Between Gender, Race, and Interaction Ritual Variables**

	Gender			Race		
	Male	Female	Difference	Non-indigenous	Indigenous	Difference
Ritual Ingredients						
Balance	3.63	4.47	−0.84**	3.83	2.86	0.97**
Stigmatization	1.89	1.54	0.35	1.78	2.23	−0.45
Defiance	2.59	2.75	−0.16	2.60	2.69	−0.09
Ritual Outcomes						
Solidarity	2.82	2.91	−0.09	2.90	2.14	0.76*
Emotional Energy	5.43	5.94	−0.51	5.50	4.37	1.13*
Reintegration	4.97	5.49	−0.43	5.13	4.17	0.96*

*p < .05; **p<.01, two tailed t-tests

suggestion arising from the qualitative data that women play a key role in the conference. Again, it should be noted that all the observation data were mostly focused on the behaviour of the offender.

We do not have the gender distributions of the entire conference but future research will seek to examine the effect, if any, of the offender's gender, as well as the effects of the gender of the victim's and offender's supporters. For instance, the qualitative results suggested that female-initiated 'turning points' were key to producing group solidarity. In the data for these conferences there were no measures for identifiable turning points so we do not know if there were any. We can hypothesize, however, on the basis of the qualitative data, that successful conferences—that is, those marked by high solidarity, reintegration, and emotional energy— were more likely to have a turning point and that these turning points were more likely to have been precipitated by a woman's participation.

This analysis also showed that conference ingredients and outcomes differed by race. Indigenous offenders were less likely to have a balanced conference than non-indigenous offenders. However, levels of stigmatization towards offenders or acts of defiance within conferences did not differ by race. This raised interesting questions regarding the dynamics of conferences in which offenders were indigenous. Conference outcomes also differed by race, with the conferences of indigenous offenders resulting in significantly lower levels of solidarity, emotional energy, and reintegration than non-indigenous offenders. This suggests that the dynamics of conferences play out differently with indigenous offenders (and white police officers as facilitators).

As stated earlier, previous analysis of the RISE data indicated different levels of reoffending for indigenous and non-indigenous offenders (Sherman, Strang, and Woods, 2004). This suggests there was something qualitatively different about the dynamics of the conferences that generated these outcomes. The different outcomes have been interpreted as an instance where indigenous offenders had a 'defiant' reaction to the (white) police authority running the conferences (Sherman, Strang, and Woods, 2004). However, there was no difference in levels of defiance as captured by the observation instrument between white and indigenous offenders. This may be due to the small number of indigenous people in this sample (n = 13). It may also be the case that defiant reactions to a conference develop over time and cannot be measured with this data. However, the measures with which to test this hypothesis are not available. What is known is that while there was no difference in defiance, there was a significant difference in ritual outcomes. This could be because indigenous offenders are being treated differently, or they experience conferencing differently, or it could indicate that better measures are needed to capture the ritual ingredients that contributed to this difference. These relationships will be examined further in the multivariate results analysis.

Multivariate results

Beginning with group solidarity (Table 6.7), age is positively associated with increased levels of solidarity in restorative justice conferences, but when the interaction ritual ingredients are added to the model, the effect is reduced by three per cent and becomes non-significant. Similarly, neither race nor gender variables produced significant results in either model one or model two.

There are strong independent effects of the interaction ritual ingredients on group solidarity with an expected negative relationship between stigmatization and defiance, and group solidarity. Although both of these variables reduced solidarity in a conference, defiance reduced solidarity by twelve per cent more than acts of stigmatization. However, a surprising non-significant finding was the lack of association between balance and solidarity.

Table 6.7 Standardized Regression Coefficients Predicting Solidarity

	Model 1		Model 2	
Male	−0.12	(0.30)	−0.05	(0.28)
Non-indigenous	0.16	(0.35)	0.08	(0.31)
Age	0.20*	(0.04)	0.17	(0.04)
Balance			0.17	(0.09)
Stigmatization			−0.25***	(0.10)
Defiance			−0.37***	(0.07)
N	107		107	
Adjusted R-sq	0.067		0.302	

Note: Standard errors in parentheses

*p< 0.05, **p<0.01, ***p<0.001

I originally hypothesized that balance would be a key concept for predicting interactional success. However, if we refer back to the video analysis of the conference discussed in Chapter Four, that conference was not balanced by these measures—the offender's wife dominated the conference and the rest of the participants only gave minimal input—and yet it was a successful interaction ritual with genuine expressions of solidarity. The items used to measure balance included a quantitative assessment of the amount of time an offender spoke and how much they contributed, so perhaps this quantitative construct did not quite capture the dynamics of an emotionally and rhythmically balanced conference. Finally, statistical interactions between a number of variables were tested, but produced no significant results, and are not reported here.

For reintegration, the results in Table 6.8 show that while gender, race, and age are not associated with reintegration, the interaction ritual ingredients have a significant impact on this outcome. Balance increases the level of reintegration, and stigmatization and defiance decreases it.

The effects of balance on reintegration differed by race and gender, and I reported separate models examining the interactions

Table 6.8 Standardized Regression Coefficients Predicting Reintegration

	Model 1		Model 2		Model 3		Model 4	
Male	−0.15	(−0.45)	−0.02	(0.39)	−0.60*	(0.38)	−0.03	(1.22)
Non-indigenous	0.18	(0.51)	0.07	(0.42)	0.05	(0.99)	−0.37	(0.41)
Age	0.04	(0.06)	−0.04	(0.05)	−0.08	(0.05)	−0.05	(0.05)
Balance			0.29**	(0.12)	−0.06	(0.57)	−0.75	(0.23)
Stigmatization			−0.34***	(0.14)	−0.33***	(0.13)	−0.38***	(0.13)
Defiance			−0.34***	(0.09)	−0.33***	(0.09)	−0.29***	(0.09)
Balance*male					0.63*	(0.27)		
Balance* indigenous							1.24*	(0.30)
N	107		107		107		107	
Adjusted R-sq	0.031		0.365		0.396		0.393	

Note: Standard errors in parentheses

*p< 0.05, **p<0.01, ***p<0.001

Table 6.9 Standardized Regression Coefficients Predicting Emotional Energy

	Model 1		Model 2	
Male	−0.18	(0.47)	−0.04	(0.47)
Non-indigenous	0.10	(0.53)	0.03	(0.51)
Age	0.32**	(0.06)	0.21*	(0.06)
Balance			0.31**	(0.14)
Stigmatization			−0.18*	(0.16)
Defiance			0.08	(0.11)
N	107		107	
Adjusted R-sq	0.127		0.229	

Note: Standard errors in parentheses

*p< 0.05, **p<0.01, ***p<0.001

between balance and gender, and balance and race. In model three, we see that once the interaction term is added, the main effect of balance becomes non-significant, although the main effects of gender and the interaction of gender and balance were significant. This can be interpreted to mean that men, on average, had less reintegrative conferences, and that balanced conferences with male offenders produced less reintegration than balanced conferences with female offenders. Also, when race was interacted with balance, we saw no main effects of race or balance, but a positive coefficient for the interaction of the two, suggesting that conferences with indigenous offenders that were marked by conversational balance, perhaps meaning that everyone had a chance to speak, were more reintegrative than balanced conferences between white offenders and victims.

Finally, in relation to emotional energy, Table 6.9 shows that age is associated with increased levels of emotional energy. That is, for each additional year of age of an offender, emotional energy increased by thirty-two per cent. However, it may be that the measures for emotional energy—slouching, sullen, hiding behaviour—would tend to decrease the further one progresses from adolescence. When ritual ingredients were added to the model, the effect of age remained significant but this reduced by eleven per cent.

Both the balance and stigmatization variables were significant in the expected direction but there was no significant relationship with defiance. This finding replicated the bivariate results that showed no relationship between emotional energy and defiance—a logically intuitive finding. Interaction terms were also added to the model but produced no significant results and so are not included here.

Conclusion

This chapter has further examined the micro dynamics of a restorative justice conference to provide an in-depth look at ritual outcomes and an empirical model that connects ritual ingredients to outcomes. The findings support ritual theories in a number of ways. Conferences that were subjectively defined by facilitators as their most 'successful' also contained the elements of a successful interaction ritual. There was a build-up of emotional intensity in the time leading up to the conference and, while the conferences may initially have been disjointed or lacking rhythm, facilitators and participants relied on a number of strategies to create mutual entrainment and a rhythmic exchange of words.

There is generally at least one emotional high point in a successful conference, where participants begin to show physical signs of high solidarity that were not there before, for example, sustained eye contact, touching, and laughing. Furthermore, a quantitative analysis of systematic observations of restorative justice conferences revealed distinct dimensions of ritual ingredients and outcomes such as balance, rhythm, and solidarity. When combined in a statistical model, the elements of an interaction ritual successfully predict positive outcomes such as solidarity, reintegration, and emotional energy. This moves the argument away from a focus on individual characteristics and towards situational dynamics.

An important finding in this analysis is the lack of support for the influence of demographic characteristics on a ritually successful conference. With the exception of reintegration, individual characteristics do not influence ritual outcomes once situational dynamics of the conference are added to the model. For the reintegration outcome, while gender and race may mediate the effects of balance on reintegration, care should be taken in drawing too strong a conclusion as the number of both women and indigenous people in these data was so small. Furthermore, almost all of the indigenous offenders in this sample were male (there were only two indigenous females), which may make some of the findings about race and gender less reliable.

This data provides preliminary support for interaction ritual theory in restorative justice. The unique data captured in systematic observations has provided an opportunity to attempt to model and test interaction ritual variables. While the data represents the best approximations available of interaction ritual, it is imperfect and important concepts from the qualitative analysis—such as the role of turning points or symbolic representations of shared morality and solidarity—were not able to be measured. Hopefully, future research can remedy this.

The findings do, however, push forward the micro agenda and elevate the importance of situational variables over the traditional individual characteristics used in criminological research, namely, the differences arising due to race, gender, and age. This suggests that the micro dynamics of interaction may be more important variables than individual characteristics—this will be further explored in Chapter Seven.

There are limitations when translating the elements of interaction ritual to quantitative analysis, mainly because an interaction ritual is, for the most part, a feedback process where ingredients produce results that produce more ingredients for further interaction rituals. This feedback process was captured through the micro analysis of the conference video in Chapter Four. To translate this to a linear model may oversimplify a complex series of causes and effects.

When doing this type of analysis we need to keep this in mind and constantly critique our methods. These theoretical and empirical problems make the case for multi method research even stronger. The holes or simplifications that the quantitative analysis leaves us with can be remedied and supplemented by the qualitative and video analyses, which problematize these concepts and patterns, and provide a fuller picture of how interaction rituals and emotions work in restorative justice conferences.

The results are very promising and contribute to the development of a comprehensive theory of restorative justice. However, a key part of restorative justice research is focused on its impact on reoffending and I have argued earlier that generalized comparisons of restorative justice to traditional courtroom justice are not very useful, and understanding variations within conferences may be the most effective way to evaluate offending (see Hayes and Daly, 2003, 2004). So, the natural next question is how does interaction ritual influence offending behaviour? If a successful ritual produces solidarity and emotional energy in the short-term, what about long-term effects? Does the emotional energy produced in a conference influence a person's behaviour in the long-term? Is the best indicator of long-term levels of emotional energy a commitment to stop offending? Are ritually successful conferences more likely to reduce offending than less emotionally rich conferences? These empirical questions will be addressed in Chapter Seven.

The interaction ritual model makes important theoretical advancements which put micro sociology to the forefront of restorative justice theory and research. There is much fine-tuning to be done to further develop a comprehensive theory of restorative justice. For instance, the current analysis is heavily skewed towards the offender. We do not know how this interaction ritual works from the victim's perspective. We have measures of the short-term emotional energy of the offender, but not the victim. Future refinements will address this.

7

Long-Term Consequences of Successful Interaction Rituals

Interaction ritual theory has the capacity to refine our understanding of how restorative justice works and provide the tools to measure, qualitatively and quantitatively, the micro dynamics of a restorative justice conference. Conferences that have the right ritual ingredients can produce positive outcomes such as group solidarity, emotional energy, and reintegration. But a common question restorative justice researchers and practitioners ask is: do these outcomes lead to a reduction in reoffending?

In this chapter, I examine the long-term effects of restorative justice. The qualitative research shows how conferences can vary in terms of their emotional quality and micro interactional success. Along with Hayes and Daly (2003) and Shapland and colleagues (2008), I suggest that an understanding of these variations provides a useful evaluation tool. Therefore, instead of broadly comparing restorative justice with non-restorative (court) justice, I analyse in micro terms how the quality and conditions of the restorative justice conference may have an influence on long-term offending behaviour.

While there is qualitative evidence that a restorative justice conference can act as a turning point in an offender's life, the following analysis will quantitatively test this proposition. Having sketched a theoretical model using qualitative interviews and micro analysis of conferences, I then translated this to quantitative data, further refined the key concepts, and conducted an initial test of the short-term effects of an interaction ritual in order to provide preliminary evidence for this model. In this chapter, I will address further the issue of how micro variations in restorative justice can influence offending in order to develop a comprehensive theory of interaction ritual in restorative justice.

Why Study Reoffending?

There is an ongoing debate within the restorative justice community about what restorative justice can, and should, achieve (Robinson and Shapland, 2008). On the one hand, if the aim of restorative justice is to restore victims, offenders, and communities, then the process is a success if it provides emotional healing, restoration, or compensation. On the other hand, others argue that if restorative justice is to be taken seriously as a viable component of the justice process then it needs to reduce reoffending. While both claims have their merit, I argue that, in either case, we need a better way of understanding the dynamics of conferencing in order to best evaluate its outcomes. A framework grounded in ritual theory can provide such a method.

This ideological debate over restorative justice outcomes can at times overlap with larger methodological debates in criminological research, with qualitative researchers focusing on the process and dynamics of conferencing, and quantitative criminologists conducting research that statistically compares conferencing with courts. These two perspectives have become increasingly fractured and unable to communicate with each other. On the one hand, quantitative criminologists tend to disregard the work of qualitative criminologists due to lack of generalizability, replicability, or similar concerns, while qualitative criminologists tend to see statisticians as mindlessly churning out numbers that don't have any deep meaning or relevance to people's actual experiences. This debate is growing especially fierce in a climate where 'evidence-based practice' is increasingly becoming a component of justice policy—where 'evidence' largely means a reduction in recidivism and increase in economic efficiency.

I argue that criminological theory can play a role in moderating these tensions. Both qualitative and quantitative approaches can address fundamental sociological and criminological questions about justice dynamics and outcomes. An exclusive focus on recidivism results in research that broadly compares restorative justice to court outcomes—a blunt measure for such a complex process. At the same time, a thick and deep description of emotions, while perhaps insightful, can also be seen as indulgent. However, an analysis of how emotions and ritual can be related to subsequent offending provides a possibility for engagement with 'evidence-based' policy-makers. Rather than another comparison of how restorative justice compares to court, a *theoretically driven* analysis that lays out the conditions under which restorative justice can impact offending is welcome.

At the same time, using the dominant discourse of 'evidence-based policy' that emphasizes reoffending over other outcomes can delegitimize many other equally valuable consequences that a restorative justice process may offer, such as opening up a dialogue between victim and offender, providing a space for restoration or healing, or offering a chance to participate directly in the justice process. It would be a mistake to privilege reoffending over these other outcomes. As such, I present this analysis as an empirical test of a theoretically driven hypothesis that participation in different types of interaction rituals can have long-term benefits, one of which is reduced offending.

Measuring Reoffending

Reoffending measures are drawn from the official arrest histories of offenders in the Reintegrative Shaming Experiments ('RISE') study (Sherman et al, 1998).[1] Every six months for up to five years after random assignment into the conference group, the Australian Federal Police reported all arrests to the RISE researchers.[2] They also reported all arrests in the five years prior to random assignment as a baseline measure. The arrests were coded into three groups: offences against a personal victim, police-detected offences, and offences committed as a defiant reaction to authority.[3]

Offences against a personal victim ('OPV') include traditional personal and property crimes such as burglary, theft, and assault. Police-detected offences ('PDO') are statutory offences and violations that resulted in an arrest, for example, driving violations. The third group, offences committed as a defiant reaction to authority ('DRA'), includes arrests for offences committed in direct defiance of authority such as failure to appear at a court hearing or violation of the conditions of probation.

The current analysis focuses on reoffending in the personal victim category. Interaction ritual theory emphasizes the personal

---

[1] The RISE study is discussed in detail in Chapters Three and Six of this book.

[2] There is a short time lag between the date of randomization and the date of the conference, generally a few weeks.

[3] Dan Woods, RISE Data Analyst, created and coded these groups.

connections made during interactions and it is, therefore, reasonable to assume that if restorative justice has a deterrent effect, it will be for offences against a personal victim. This is consistent with other research in criminology that evaluates criminal justice interventions, such as the effectiveness of drug courts by measuring arrests for drug offences, or the effectiveness of sex-offender therapy by measuring arrests for sex offences. An arrest due to a driving violation or technical violation of probation conditions may not be an accurate indicator of a restorative justice motivated commitment to stop offending.[4]

In the criminological literature there are two well-documented ways to measure offending: prevalence measures and frequency measures. Prevalence measures look at whether a person was rearrested or not, and frequency measures look at the number (or rate) of arrests over time. A prevalence measure is a more conservative measure, while a frequency measure allows for 'mistakes' on the path to desistance. The following analysis examines both prevalence and frequency outcomes.

Figure 7.1 shows the percentage of personal victim offenders who were rearrested over five years. Within six months of their random assignment to the restorative justice group, 17.2 per cent of offenders were rearrested and this percentage steadily grew to 44.8 per cent over five years. While the prevalence data shows that almost half of the offenders reoffended, the frequency data indicates that most were rearrested only once.

Table 7.1 shows the frequency of arrest for offenders in this sample. About fifty-five per cent of offenders were not rearrested, eighteen per cent were arrested once, about sixteen per cent were arrested between two and five times, and the remaining ten per cent were arrested more than five times.

Predicting reoffending

In Chapter Six, the outcome variables in the analysis were the interaction ritual outcomes created through confirmatory factor analysis. The analysis showed how the positive ritual outcomes of solidarity, reintegration, and emotional energy were produced.

---

[4] However, I also repeated the analysis looking at all types of arrests as an outcome variable. There was no difference at all between the two types of reoffending data and I do not include it here.

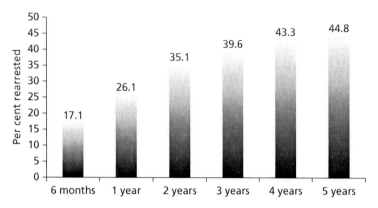

Figure 7.1 Arrest Prevalence Over Five Years

Table 7.1 Arrest Frequencies Five Years After the Experiment

No. of arrests	Frequency	Per cent
0	74	55.2
1	24	17.9
2	7	5.2
3	9	6.7
4	1	0.8
5	5	3.7
6-10	5	3.7
11-20	6	4.5
Over 20	3	2.2
Total	*134*	*100.00*

In this chapter, three ritual outcomes will be used to predict the prevalence and frequency of reoffending: solidarity (the interpersonal connections between victim and offender), reintegration (the support and connections between the offender), and their supporters), and emotional energy (a generalized measure of the offender's emotional state at the time).

Control variables include the demographic characteristics used in Chapter Six. As the mean age for offenders in the study was about sixteen years old, the majority did not have long offence histories.

Table 7.2 summarizes the arrest frequencies of participants in the year prior to the restorative justice conference. Fifty-eight per cent had no arrests in the year prior to their conference, which suggests that, for many of them, the arrest and resulting conference was their first interaction with the criminal justice system. A further 28.4 per cent had one arrest prior to their conference and the remainder (fourteen per cent) had been arrested between two and five times previously. Because such a large percentage of offenders had no prior history, and most of those who did had a record of only one arrest, the measure of prevalence of an arrest for a personal victim offence was limited to the year prior to random assignment as a control variable.[5]

Even if we agree that emotions and interactions are at the core of social life, is it plausible that a very intense, emotionally powerful, two hour restorative justice conference could influence an offender's future behaviour for years after the interaction? Drawing on interaction ritual theory, I hypothesize that powerful interaction rituals may have a long-term impact on a person's behaviour and that conferences with high levels of solidarity, emotional energy, and reintegration would be related to less offending than conferences with lower levels of these variables. I further propose that while individual level control variables do not influence reoffending once the interaction ritual variables are added to the model,

Table 7.2 Arrest Frequencies One Year Prior to Random Assignment

No. of Arrests	Frequency	Per cent
0	78	58.2
1	38	28.4
2	6	4.5
3	7	5.2
4	3	2.2
5	2	31.5
Total	134	100.0

[5] Prior arrest data was made available by the Australian Federal Police for up to five years prior to random assignment; however, the mean age of offenders was only sixteen years old and most of their prior histories were in the year before their conference. Thus, although this analysis was run with two-, three-, four, and five-year histories as a control, this did not alter the results.

an offender's prior history will remain a strong predictor of future offending.

In criminological research, prior offending has consistently been a strong indicator of future offending and, accordingly, I assume that this is unlikely to change as a result of the addition of interaction ritual variables. Also, unlike individual level variables such as race, gender, and age, an offender's prior history of arrest(s) may mean they have participated in previous solidarity and emotional energy building, or deducting, interaction rituals that are still influencing behaviour.

I use both prevalence and frequency of arrest to examine bivariate and multivariate relationships between reoffending and restorative justice as well as the relationship between interaction ritual outcomes and the prevalence of arrests. I then explore how interaction ritual variables influence the frequency of arrests. Due to the skewed nature of the arrest frequencies (over half of the sample were not rearrested), a combination of statistical tests have been used to make these comparisons and ascertain whether there is a statistically significant difference between groups.[6]

The skewed nature of the data presents a challenge to multivariate analysis. Traditionally, a poisson regression would be used to account for this. However, this data has a very high number of people who are never rearrested and, because of this, an ordinary poisson distribution would underpredict zero counts in a regression model. Therefore, to address this, a Zero-Inflated Poisson ('ZIP') regression model was used (Lambert, 1992). This model assumed the presence of two latent groups in the data: those who will never be rearrested (with an arrest count of zero and probability of one) and those whose distribution of arrests will follow a traditional poisson distribution (that is, where most offenders will be rearrested a small number of times, with a small group of high reoffending offenders). Thus, this analysis reports two sets of coefficients—a probability of being in the zero-arrest group and, for those in the second group, a poisson coefficient estimating the likelihood of arrest frequency (Long and Freese, 2006).[7]

---

[6] Mann-Whitney U Tests and Median Tests are two ways to statistically compare the differences between groups. They are considered non-parametric tests, which means that they are most appropriate when the data does not follow a normal distribution, as in this case.

[7] In addition, ZIP models are susceptible to overdispersion, where the observed variance exceeds that which is predicted by the model. Vuong (1989) provides a

I take a multistep approach to modelling for interaction ritual in restorative justice and reoffending. This involves presenting a bivariate analysis of the relationship between prior arrests on future offending and then running a second model with the individual level control variables added. Following that, the interaction ritual variables are added to the model. Finally, I present a series of models with different interaction terms, in which significant interactions only are reported. In each stage, raw coefficients are reported for the count models, and probabilities are reported for the logistic models. To help interpret these statistics, I provide exponentiated coefficients and describe what they mean.

Relationships Between Ritual Outcomes and Reoffending

The results of the bivariate relationship between interaction ritual outcomes and arrest prevalence are presented in Table 7.3. It shows that solidarity and reintegration are significantly related to whether or not a participant is rearrested and higher mean levels of solidarity and reintegration in the conference are correlated with cases where offenders are not rearrested. The results, however, do not suggest a relationship between emotional energy and rearrest.

Table 7.3 Bivariate Relationship Between Interaction Ritual Variables and Arrest Prevalence

	Arrest Prevalence		Difference
	0	1	
Mean solidarity	3.04	2.57	0.47*
Mean emotional energy	5.26	5.35	0.27
Mean reintegration	5.44	4.54	0.90**

N = 124; *p<.05, **p<.01, ***p<.001, two tailed test

statistic to test the fit of the data to a ZIP model compared to an ordinary poisson model. In general, Vuong scores that are higher than 1.96 favour the ZIP model over the poisson model. I report the Vuong statistics with my results.

Table 7.4 presents the results of two different bivariate tests of interaction ritual and arrest frequency. To do this analysis, the interaction ritual variables (solidarity, reintegration, and emotional energy) were dichotomized and used as a comparison group to mean arrest frequency.[8] This meant that conferences were rated 'high' or 'low' on each of these interaction variables depending on whether they scored above or below the mean score. For instance, a conference that scored above the mean would be considered to have 'high solidarity' and such conferences resulted in significantly fewer arrests after five years. This was true for the median test and the Mann-Whitney U Test for skewed data. There were similar results for reintegration, with highly reintegrative conferences significantly related to less offending. However, similar to the prevalence measures, there was no relationship between emotional energy and frequency of offending.

Table 7.4 Relationship Between Interaction Ritual Outcomes and Arrest Frequency

| | Mann-Whitney U tests | | | |
	Mean arrests	Standard dev.	Z	Prob.
Solidarity				
Low	3.09	5.98		
High	1.07	2.46		
Difference	2.01*		2.7	0.007
Emotional energy				
Low	2.74	5.98		
High	1.83	3.95		
Difference	0.91		0.3	0.77
Reintegration				
Low	2.78	5.19		
High	1.58	4.37		
Difference	1.19**		3.14	0.002

N = 124; *p<.05, **p<.01, two sided median test

[8] The mean is reported for comparison in the table, but the statistical tests are of the median and the distribution of arrest.

Moving to the multivariate analysis, the story becomes more complicated. Table 7.5 presents the multistep ZIP model.[9] In addition, the inflated (logit) model which predicted membership in the non-arrest group produced no significant results for the interaction

Table 7.5 Zero-Inflated Regression Coefficients for Five Year Reoffending

	Model 1		Model 2		Model 3		Model 4	
Count model (frequency)								
Prior prevalence	−0.19	(0.12)	−0.01	(0.14)	0.02	(0.17)	1.98***	(0.46)
Male			1.12**	(0.36)	1.02**	(0.35)	1.47***	(0.37)
Age			−0.25***	(0.04)	−0.23***	(0.04)	−0.24***	(0.05)
Non-indigenous			−0.52**	(0.16)	−0.61***	(0.17)	−0.72***	(0.17)
Solidarity					−0.39***	(0.10)	−0.28**	(0.10)
Emotional energy					−0.01	(0.04)	0.07	(0.05)
Reintegration					0.18***	(0.05)	0.36***	(0.06)
Reint* priors							−0.43***	(0.09)
Inflated model (prevalence)								
Prior prevalence	−1.43***	(0.38)	−1.10*	(0.46)	−1.09	(0.52)	−1.62	(1.81)
Male			−0.39	(0.78)	−0.32	(0.82)	0.20	(1.00)
Age			0.12	(0.12)	0.17	(0.13)	0.15	(0.13)
Non-indigenous			1.10	(0.76)	1.19	(0.82)	1.16	(0.85)
Solidarity					−0.23	(0.32)	−0.25	(0.33)
Emotional energy					−0.15	(0.15)	−0.14	(0.15)
Reintegration					0.40	(0.22)	0.34	(0.28)
Reint* priors							0.07	(2.61)
N	134		111		107		107	
chi2	2.44		135.28		138.23		161.95	
Vuong	2.95		3.39		3.33		3.63	

Standard errors in parentheses; *p<0.05, **p<0.01, ***p<0.001

[9] The Vuong statistic suggests that the data fit the ZIP model over the poisson model. However, I also estimated models using traditional poisson regression, and

ritual variables. In the first three models, having a prior history predicted membership in the non-zero, or rearrest, group. Once the interaction term was added in model four, however, prior history lost significance in the logit model (although this may be an artefact of the non-significant interaction term).

The count model produced a number of interesting results. First, the prevalence of prior arrests in the year before random assignment to the conference did not predict the frequency of future arrest. The three individual level control variables all significantly influenced arrest counts, even after the interaction ritual variables were added to the model. In general, it showed that being male, young, and indigenous strongly influenced arrest frequency, independent of other factors.

Similar to the bivariate analysis, both solidarity and reintegration influenced future offending counts, but emotional energy had no effect on future behaviour. Conferences with high solidarity were significantly related to less offending at five years, but conferences that were highly reintegrative actually resulted in more offending at five years.

While this finding is initially puzzling, it helps to examine the ways the different variables relate to each other. This is accomplished by including an interaction term in the model which helps to disentangle the relationship between the controls and the independent variables. The only significant interaction was between prior offending prevalence and reintegration—having a prior offending history changed the direction of the influence of integration. Where an offender had no arrest history, and had a highly reintegrative conference, offending increased; but where they had an offending history, and experienced a reintegrative conference, offending decreased. This finding will be discussed further in this chapter.

By reporting the per cent changes in reoffending frequency for each variable, Table 7.6 helps to interpret the data. Examining the data in this way makes clear the strength of the interaction ritual variables. While individual characteristics such as gender, age, and race have an impact on the frequency of future offending, so too do the situational variables such as the amount of solidarity expressed at the conference as well as the reintegration-prior

produced coefficients with similar significance levels and directions, which suggests that this is the best statistical test to be using.

Table 7.6 Interpretation of Coefficients in Count Model

	b	Exp (b)	Per cent change
Prevalence of priors	1.95	7.25	624.7
Male	1.47	4.37	336.5
Age	−0.24	0.79	−21.3
Non-indigenous	−0.72	0.49	−51.2
Solidarity	−0.28	0.76	−24.6
Emotional energy	0.07	1.08	7.8
Reintegration	0.36	1.43	42.9
Reintegration * priors	−0.43	0.65	−34.9

Exp(b) = factor change for unit increase in x
Per cent change = per cent change in expected count for unit increase in x

offending interaction of variables discussed earlier. For example, for a unit change in solidarity, arrest count decreased by 24.6 per cent, and for the reintegration-prior history interaction offending decreased by 34.9 per cent. Being male increased the arrest count by 336.5 per cent, and being non-indigenous decreased offending by 51.2 per cent. Finally, for each year of age, the expected arrest count decreased by 21.3 per cent.

These findings give rise to a number of interesting points for discussion. The ZIP model allows us to examine both the prevalence and frequency of arrest as a dependent variable and, with the exception of prior history, most of the variables were not significant for the prevalence model. It seems that the key interaction ritual variables will not influence whether or not a person reoffends at all but, if one is likely to be arrested, then these variables will influence the frequency of arrest.

Emotional Energy in the Short- and Long-Term

Contrary to my original hypothesis, emotional energy in the restorative justice conference was not found to be a significant variable related to reoffending. However, this finding may be due to the way emotional energy is measured in this data. Emotional energy has both short- and long-term aspects and while the measures capture the transient component of emotional energy, they do not measure its long-term state (Collins, 1990). Physical cues for emotional energy such as the offender's demeanour—for example, stuttering, slouching, and 'hiding' behaviour—provide measures of emotional energy at a conference, but long-term emotional energy states are more likely than these short-term emotional snapshots to be a predictor of offending. These long-term measures of an offender's emotional energy are able to be captured in longitudinal interviews or observations.

Emotional energy may be fleeting and may decay when not reinforced by subsequent interactions. For example, in interviews conducted two years after a restorative justice conference, it was clear that some offenders were still feeling its residual effects. Specifically, this was in cases where the offender had participated in successful rituals that resulted in expressed feelings of pride about their participation, a sense of morals, and trust in the police as a result of their interaction.

Expressions of pride were a common result of a successful restorative justice conference. Participants saw themselves as special and especially courageous, they even revelled in the scepticism of others such as when one offender told his mother about the conference. Her response was, 'So now you want to be on Jerry Springer next?' This response, which suggested she believed the conference was all show and no substance, did not deter the offender and he confided knowingly, 'She didn't understand, how could she understand?' Since his mother did not attend the conference, she didn't have the insider knowledge of a group member and could not be a part of the collective experience.

Another offender recounted a similar story in relation to a conversation with a cellmate about the conference. The cellmate told him, 'You've got to be mad,' and the offender responded, 'Well I had a reason why I done it.' As he recounted in an interview, 'It's none of his business. It didn't really matter what he said.' He took pride in being different from those around him and enjoyed a special status that the experience of participating in restorative justice brought him.

Emotional energy also parallels Durkheim's notion of 'moral sentiment'. According to Collins, 'Persons who are full of emotional energy feel like good persons; they feel righteous about what they are doing' (Collins, 2004: 109). This can be seen in the narrative of Paul, a forty-year-old heroin addict who had spent nearly eighteen years behind bars before his conference. Two years after his restorative justice conference, and subsequent prison sentence, he described feeling good about his new status as a law-abiding citizen,

[Restorative justice] played a big big major part in my life, a big major part. To the point where we have another friend, and he recently relapsed, he started using drugs again. And when he first started, we brought him over to stay at ours, to try and help him. And he went out and went missing, and we found him at the pub. But in between that period, he was missing for a couple of hours, I was worried that he was gonna commit a crime, and I was gonna have to tell him that if I found out he committed a crime, that I would have to tell the police. That was coming from me. Yeah, there was me who's been a crook all his life, but I would have to tell the police, because that is the right thing to do.

Paul was able to appreciate and reflect on how much he had changed including registering his surprise at this change in sentiment, which would have been unheard of in his earlier life. During his narrative, he described how he now feels good about the respect and autonomy he enjoys in his job, in the loving relationship he has with a new partner, and in his newfound commitment to mentoring younger offenders. This is consistent with research by Maruna (2001), who examined narratives of desistance among a sample of ex-offenders. Maruna found that ex-offenders develop a 'redemption narrative', or a story they can tell themselves that is consistent with a new identity they are trying to project. In this case, Paul uses his experience in restorative justice to create a self-narrative of redemption.

Finally, and importantly from a procedural justice perspective, emotional energy can lead to a newfound trust in the police. A number of offenders described their surprise at how objective the police facilitator was during the conference and agreed that they had never been treated so well by a police officer before. Asked about the facilitator in his case, Paul said, 'Oh I love him. A lovely man, he's a good man. He's got a wealth of experience. If it wasn't for [facilitator], I probably wouldn't be sitting here today.' When asked to elaborate, he went on,

When I first met [facilitator], my barrier's up. Because he's a policeman. And I've never had a mate who's a policeman, they've always been the enemy. And, don't trust a policeman, they'll fit you up or beat you up, one of the two. But as I've come to know him, well he's gonna be my best man for god sake, you know? So that says it all, doesn't it, that says it all.

It may be that the observations made during the conference are not the best indicators of emotional energy or its long-term effects and that the long-term emotional state is best measured through interviews and observations at a later date.

Emotional Energy for Facilitators

The measures of emotional energy used above are offender focused. The findings from the quantitative analysis suggest that the measures I have used to conceptualize emotional energy may not be accurate, and that a qualitative investigation of this concept is more useful. While future research will explore this more deeply, there is preliminary evidence from my interviews that facilitators are getting an emotional energy boost from restorative justice as well. In fact, a ritual theory would predict that they benefit the most, as they get to repeat the interaction ritual every time they convene a conference. The facilitators I spoke to worked extremely hard and were professionally and emotionally invested in producing high quality conferences. This was demonstrated during our interviews, when they would become visibly upset at the memory of an unsuccessful conference, and sometimes tear up at the memory of their best one. They spoke of being profoundly impacted through exposure to the emotions that offenders and victims expressed in a conference. This was a different kind of ritual to what they were used to as police officers. As one facilitator explained,

When I heard [in the conference] about the effects that [the crime] had on the victim, my eyes were red and puffy. I found it quite emotional. After having been carrying around in the streets for god knows how many years, and being a policeman's policeman, or a roughty tufty, or whatever you want to call it, to be sitting down with nothing but raw emotions coming from people, it was something that I have not encountered before. Obviously I've been in someone's house before and they've been crying, and everybody's crying, there's a lot of emotion. But this was totally different. This was people exorcising some real heavyweight shit. Lifechanging stuff.

Another facilitator described how the job continues to renew their faith in humanity.

You kind of take ownership of these things. That's how it affects me anyway. However the conference progresses you feel a certain responsibility towards the people. You brought them all together, sometimes under pretty adverse circumstances. Then they come together and talk it out and they trust you to see them through it…you have to trust the people to come to a solution together. Most of the time your trust is well founded because they can and they do. But you can't help but be affected by how they do. It reinforces your faith in human nature in certain cases. There are pretty crumby people out there who do some pretty harmful things. And you get them together under these circumstances and you see that they're quite decent, and you are quite surprised.

At the same time, this type of work can be extremely draining on facilitators. Facilitators describe feeling 'deflated', 'exhausted', 'drained', and 'worn out' after a conference. This is consistent with other occupations that require a large amount of emotional labour in order to pull off a successful interaction (Hochschild, 1983; Collins, 2004). As one facilitator explained,

I wasn't ready for it. I found it quite emotional. When I walked out of prison that day and said my goodbyes to everybody and got in my car with [observer] I was ripped. I found the drive home really difficult, I couldn't concentrate. I was tired, as I am after most conferences. I found that I had expended so much mental energy and mental power that all I wanted to do was just sit in the car and just drive, not have to speak. But obviously [observer] was in the car and wanted to have a conversation about the conference, how we thought it went. She really was effervescent over it. I was too, but I was just really really tired.

Finally, facilitators use the emotional energy they get from good conferences to give them confidence and motivate them for future conferences. All the facilitators I spoke to had a distinct feeling of pride in their work. When telling me about his most successful conference, one facilitator recalled,

It gave me more confidence to do what I was doing. It was one of the very first robberies and I was still quite new. This was only a few months after I started, it gave me a lot of confidence to carry on with it. And they made me feel good about doing what I was doing.

Dimensions of Solidarity and Reintegration

It is clear from the results that there are distinct differences and similarities between solidarity and reintegration. Solidarity captures the positive connections made between the victim, the offender, and their supporters. It includes classic measures of group cohesiveness such as touching and crying, as well as the amount of explicit or implicit remorse and forgiveness expressed by group members. All of these items encompass a strong ritual of redemption within the group, which is consistent with the models of emotional transformation discussed by Braithwaite (1989), Scheff and Retzinger (1991), and Collins (2004), or even Maruna's (2001) model of redemptive narratives. Solidarity is akin to Scheff's 'acknowledged shame' or Braithwaite's 'reintegrative shame' or 'learned conscience'. In the micro analysis of the conference discussed in Chapter Four, the image of Aaron and Anne shaking hands and smiling captures perfectly the components of solidarity as they are measured in the quantitative data. No doubt a RISE researcher observing that conference would rate it at the high end of solidarity.

Successful interaction ritual produces this solidarity between groups which acts as a protective factor against offending. The data confirmed this hypothesis by showing that a one unit increase in group solidarity in a two hour conference reduces the frequency of arrest over five years by nearly twenty-five per cent. This provides strong evidence that the micro components of interaction are the key to understanding the potential of restorative justice as a tool to reduce crime. In other words, this finding makes it clear that a comprehensive theory of restorative justice and deterrence needs to be placed within a framework of emotions and interaction ritual.

An unexpected component in the interaction ritual model was reintegration, which was not an original part of the interaction ritual model as conceptualized by Collins (2004), but was developed inductively through the factor analysis in Chapter Six. At the outset, the intention was to develop theoretically driven measures of interaction ritual through systematic observations of solidarity and emotional energy as ritual outcomes in restorative justice conferences. However, factor analysis revealed that an additional concept was captured in the data. In an effort to be empirically rigorous and true to the data, I kept this third factor, giving the overall model the best possible fit.[10]

Reintegration encompasses the amount of love, approval, and support given to the offender by their supporters. Rather than being an indicator of overall group cohesiveness, the concept one-sidedly focuses on this pre-existing relationship. That is, it became a measure of solidarity within the group (offender and supporters) instead of a measure of solidarity between the groups (offender and victim).

---

[10] I attempted to combine solidarity and reintegration into one factor but this reduced the overall fit of the model substantially. I also combined these two variables into one solidarity-reintegration variable to be used in the regression models, but found no significant findings with this variable. This is further evidence that these are separate ritual concepts that have their own influences.

When used to predict reoffending, reintegration in a conference produced a counter-intuitive finding, that is, it appeared that having a reintegrative conference actually *increased* offending! However, when we look at how these situational variables such as reintegration are related to (or interact with) prior offending history, we find an even more puzzling result—that the combination of a prior history and reintegration works to *reduce* offending. So, if an offender has both a clean record and a reintegrative conference, they have an increased chance of reoffending, but if they have a prior history, and this is combined with a reintegrative conference, then the likelihood of offending is reduced. While this finding is initially baffling, it is ultimately consistent with the interaction ritual theory of emotional transformation through restorative justice.

One can hypothesize that a person with an arrest record has experienced a number of negative interaction rituals including a stigmatizing and emotionally draining arrest and, possibly, a court hearing and sentence. For this person, an intensely positive interaction such as can occur in a restorative justice conference may be the trigger that jars their sensibilities and provides them with their one positive experience within the criminal justice system. At the same time, if there is a reintegrative experience with their supporters, this can lead to a reconnection with loved ones and the restoration of broken bonds, which combined can impact future offending.

Compare this with someone who has not been arrested before and does not have a history of negative interaction with the law and legal authority. Because it is their first arrest, they are diverted out of prosecution and sent to a restorative conference where they have a successful, reintegrative conference in which their family tells them they are loved and supported. The outcome is that they know their family will love them unconditionally regardless of how they may have behaved. This may not be enough to prevent them from reoffending however for, unlike the prior offender, they have not had an intense, negative to positive, transformative experience. Instead, they have gone from a neutral to a positive experience, which may not be intense enough emotionally to reduce their future offending behaviour.

This is also consistent with evidence that suggests restorative justice is more likely to reduce offending with older, more serious criminals (Sherman and Strang, 2007). The common narrative is that one needs to 'hit rock bottom' before experiencing redemption. This further clarifies the relationship between prior offending history and a reintegrative conference—offenders with longer histories may be the ones who need strong positive rituals the most!

A final notable finding is that individual level control variables still strongly influence offending. This suggests that a combination of individual and situational variables guides our behaviour. However, characteristics such as gender, age, and race/ethnicity may only be shorthand for the sum of our experiences, or interaction rituals. For instance, being male is strongly related to an increase in offending. But does this mean that men are somehow inherently different to women? Or does it mean that, on average, men participate in different types of interaction rituals that are perhaps more conducive to reoffending than the types of interaction rituals women participate in? Remember that as individuals participate in social life, they enter a market for ritual solidarity (Collins, 1990) where they are constantly seeking positive interactions to charge them up. The variables used in this analysis represent only a few of the countless interaction rituals an individual participates in. The strength of the gender, age, and race/ethnicity variables may be inadvertently capturing some of these interaction rituals.

Conclusion

Micro situational factors are keys to determining the success of restorative justice and within-conference variation is a useful way to evaluate the deterrent effect of restorative justice. From a micro perspective, there are a wide variety of short-term conference outcomes but all conferences are not equal and to group them together for the purposes of comparison to some other process is a gross simplification.

The findings in this study contribute to a micro theory of restorative justice that can influence future research, policy, and practice. The good news about the role of interaction ritual in a restorative justice conference is that interaction ritual dynamics are malleable, and can be controlled. A good facilitator can ensure the right ingredients are there to create a successful conference.

I conclude by suggesting that we can make conferencing more efficient and effective if we place a larger emphasis on the provision of effective training for facilitators that includes the development of high level skills in understanding and managing the micro dynamics of emotion. A facilitator who is taught to pick up on micro facial, verbal, and paralinguistic cues, and who can control his or her own cues, can help ensure a positive interaction ritual. We know that people can be trained to have control over micro interactions, whether it is police officers interviewing a suspect (Katz, 2001) or TV talk show producers prepping guests before they go on air (Grindstaff, 2002). This same concept can be applied in facilitator training. With an increase in the number of high solidarity conferences, perhaps we could confidently present restorative justice conferences as a viable alternative to courts and prosecution where they are not seen simply as a soft option.

Finally, while these results provide a powerful argument for the important role of micro situational variables in producing long-term outcomes, a few key variables were not measured here. The qualitative analysis made clear that another important component in a successful interaction is the development of rhythmic entrainment over the course of the conference, which can be triggered by a single or a series of emotional turning points. The data used in the quantitative analysis did not have any explicit measures of rhythm or turning points, and rhythm in particular is challenging to measure with quantitative data because it is a developmental construct that takes place over time. I suggest that stigmatization and defiance can act as proxy measures of rhythm with some success; however, the development and measurement of interactional rhythm and turning points are key components of the interaction ritual model. Future data collection and analyses will consider how these central concepts are to be measured.

8
Conclusions

The restorative justice movement has the potential to change the lives of all those affected by crime. Although this practice is gaining legislative and political support across the world, research indicates that different types of conferences have different types of effects on different types of people (Sherman and Strang, 2007). Before we charge full speed ahead in developing new policy, we need to take a careful look at the structure and dynamics of conferences to determine what predicts success. I suggest that a micro sociological perspective informed by interaction ritual theory can help us to achieve this.

This research uses a three-pronged approach to understanding interaction in restorative justice conferences—an in-depth analysis of the emotional and interactional dynamics of restorative justice conferences using video data, a qualitative examination of successful and failed conferences based on interviews with facilitators, and a quantitative analysis of ritual ingredients and short- and long-term outcomes. I provide an empirical test of interaction ritual theory as well as a fine-grained analysis of variations within conferencing. Bringing a micro sociological perspective to the study of the restorative justice movement has moved us forward in developing the theory and practice of conferencing.

I have used a video recording of a single conference to provide in-depth detail of precisely how an interaction ritual works. I have probed deeply into the inner workings of a conference to illuminate the micro processes through which rhythm and entrainment develop over the course of the conference, as well as the ways solidarity and emotional energy can be expressed. This analysis has shown that even successful interaction rituals that produce solidarity and positive emotions between participants can display signs of stratifying power and status rituals in which participants vie for footing and engage in subtle tactics to raise their own status and gain the upper hand in an interaction.

Qualitative interviews with facilitators and offenders provide initial support for interaction ritual theory in restorative justice conferences. Facilitators are trained to maximize emotional intensity by preparing participants to express emotion, and follow the turn-taking rules needed to develop rhythm and emotional entrainment. I have also shown the different strategies facilitators use to encourage participants to develop rhythm and balance in a conference. Successful conferences are marked by key emotional 'turning points'—specific moments in the conference where the rhythm changes from one of conflict to one of solidarity. Conferences that successfully develop this balanced, rhythmic, emotional entrainment result in high solidarity interaction accompanied by a momentary rise in emotional energy. Interviews with conference offenders two years after their conference suggests the potential for these conferences to act as a turning point in their life, providing them with the long-term emotional energy needed to stop offending. Importantly, I have also analysed 'failed' conferences, investigating moments where the ritual fails to produce solidarity or leads to a depression in emotional energy.

Influenced by this micro level evidence, I have developed quantitative measures of interaction ritual in restorative justice and conducted formal tests of these models. Systematic observations of conferences reveal the structure of interaction ritual in restorative justice, with measurable ingredients and outcomes. I have developed measures for the key interaction ritual variables, including conversational balance, stigmatization, defiance, solidarity, reintegration, and emotional energy. Results from regression analysis show that one can predict ritual outcomes by measuring situational dynamics, while controlling for individual level demographic characteristics. This suggests that the micro process and situational dynamics of the interaction are driving its success.

Not only has the micro perspective provided us with measures to predict success in restorative justice, long-term evaluations have shown that ritually successful conferences are more likely to result in reduced offending than less successful conferences. This finding strengthens the argument made by Hayes and Daly (2003) that we need to understand within-conference variation before we can make conclusions about the crime reduction effects of restorative justice.

Outline of a Theory of Restorative Justice

These three approaches have brought us closer to a micro level theory of restorative justice. The interactional components of restorative justice are the key to understanding its potential as an emotionally powerful and transformative event. Drawing on the theoretical perspective of interaction ritual theory and the empirical results presented throughout the text, I present a sketch of this theory in Figure 8.1.

Success in restorative justice is contingent on a number of conditions and interactional ingredients. First, my qualitative interviews suggest that the facilitator needs to actively build up participants' emotions in the days, hours, and minutes leading up to a conference. The participants are informed about what to expect at the conference and facilitators encourage them to think about the effect that the crime has had on them. They prepare them to express their emotions in a respectful and non-dominating manner.

In addition to preparing the participant to engage in a successful conference, the physical space needs to be arranged with successful interaction ritual in mind. My interviews have shown the importance of adequate space, including a private room, attention to seating arrangements, etc. This works to create a Durkheimian sacred space (Durkheim, 1912), where individuals can leave the everyday realm and be transported to the ritual world.

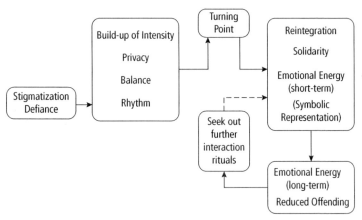

Figure 8.1 Full Model of Restorative Justice Interaction Rituals

The two most important components of a successful restorative justice ritual are the development of balance and rhythm. Balance is more than a quantitative measurement of the number of people in the room on each side or the amount of time each participant contributes.[1] Rather, it is a complex theoretical construct, consisting of both real and perceived interactional dominance. For instance, in the video discussed in Chapter Four, Gillian clearly comes to dominate the interaction. But the other participants become caught up in the rhythm and tone of her speech and align their verbal and non-verbal cues to fit hers. Her dominance does not upset the balance of the interaction, instead it leads to a common rhythm and an object of entrainment for the rest of the participants. This is qualitatively different from the road rage conference described in Chapter Five where the offender and his supporters gang up on the lone victim, causing him to apologize for being a bad driver. Because balance is closely tied to the struggle for power and status that can develop over the course of an interaction, keeping a conference balanced is a good way to help ensure success.

Rhythm is perhaps the most important element of the development of a restorative justice ritual, and no conference can be successful without it. I have used micro analysis of discourse and demeanour to show how rhythm can develop in a conference. Transcripts of a conference show how the interaction can start out disjointed with stutters, slurs, and embarrassing silences. As people warm up to each other they begin to take part in rhythmic feedback, encouraging each other with their verbal and non-verbal cues. As a rhythm develops, people become emotionally entrained with each other as they invest in the creation of a successful interaction. By putting time and effort into developing this rhythm, they hope to ensure high solidarity and emotional energy payback. I have used measures of stigmatization and defiance to represent rhythm in my quantitative analysis. These actually represent threats to rhythm, where the stigmatizing treatment of the offender, or acts of

---

[1] Indeed, when I use this overly literal definition of balance in my quantitative analysis, I find only limited support. This is not to say that there is no place for these definitions. In the systematic observations, balance as measured by the amount of time spoken and the amount the offender contributed to the conference, was significantly related to measures of reintegration and emotional energy. And, in the qualitative analysis, successful conferences had closer to equal numbers of participants on the offender's and victim's sides than failed conferences.

defiance, hinders the development of feedback or proper attention to turn-taking rules.

Successful conferences also contain one or a series of turning points, or emotional high points, where this rhythmic feedback solidifies. Such turning points are often marked by a participant displaying very strong emotions, often through crying or yelling. These moments allow the other participants to 'let their guard down', and express their emotions. These strong emotions turn the interaction into an intimate moment shared between participants. I have provided preliminary evidence to suggest that these turning points may be gendered, with female participants doing the 'emotion work' of the conference to bring about a turning point. While the quantitative data available at this time does not have such measures, this is a promising hypothesis that can be explored in future research. The emotional intensity created through these turning points further ensures balance and rhythm where, after a turning point, participants begin to display the different signs of a successful interaction.

If the right ingredients are there and we can point to one or more emotional turning points, we begin to see the outcomes of a successful conference as an interaction ritual. Participants engage in high solidarity and reintegrative behaviour. Unlike balance and rhythm, which are difficult to conceptualize in empirical terms, ritual outcomes can be easily observed and measured using both qualitative and quantitative methods. High solidarity behaviour includes people synchronizing their gesture and gaze, touching each other, hugging, and crying and laughing together. It is a measure of group cohesion that can also be measured by the exchange of emotions such as remorse, empathy, and sympathy, as well as the symbolic exchange of apology and forgiveness between offender and victim.

Reintegration is an outcome similar to solidarity, which is manifested in the quantitative data. While solidarity is a measure of whole-group cohesiveness, reintegration represents the extent to which the offender is welcomed back into a 'community of care' by loved ones or supporters. This positive outcome is a measure of emotions such as love, respect, and support between an offender and their supporters.

Positive conferences also result in a short-term boost in emotional energy. People feel charged up from this successful interaction, and become ready to seek more positive encounters. Interviews, micro observations, and systematic observations have all shown how emotional energy is externalized at a conference, for example, when participants smile more and are relaxed in their face and demeanour. They don't hide their face from others, and seem comfortable in the group. As they talk to each other, or talk to interviewers, their face lights up. Conferences that do not succeed as interaction rituals, on the other hand, are marked by feelings of deflation and disengagement. Participants literally and emotionally withdraw from the process—slouching, leaning backwards, keeping their head down, their gaze averted.

An additional hypothesized outcome is that the development of symbols represents the positive emotions produced in the conference and these collective symbols work to both store and prolong the positive ritual outcomes. Invocation of symbols can turn the positive outcomes of interaction ritual into long-term emotions. One example of this may be the outcome agreement signed by all participants, although in most cases this seems to carry little weight for the participants. Another may be through enacting the core sequence of symbolic reparation through the expression of remorse, apology, and forgiveness. This seems to carry meaning for participants, but only if the sequence feels spontaneous to them. This presents a challenge to facilitators who want to ensure the group creates moments they can take away with them as symbols, but must accept that forcing them could cause the ritual to fall flat.

The final element of the model explores the long-term effect of a successful restorative justice conference ritual. My data suggest that the positive outcomes of a conference can be sustained for years after the interaction. Key long-term outcomes include a rise in emotional energy and a reduction in offending. I have not explicitly measured long-term emotional energy, but interviews with conference participants in the days, months, and years following a conference can determine long-term emotional energy levels. However, I do present evidence that long-term emotional energy can be translated into a reduction in offending. This final step of the theory suggests that our emotions and interactions can influence our behaviour. This can happen through one's desire to maximize their stock of emotional energy by participating in more solidarity-creating rituals. In this way, a successful restorative justice conference becomes one in a series of interaction ritual chains that guide one's actions.

Future Research and Evaluation

While I present data that helps us understand the micro dynamics of conferencing, there is still much more work to be done in developing various avenues for future theory, research, and evaluation of restorative justice. First, I propose more research on the emotional dynamics and interaction ritual outcomes for all participants. This analysis has focused mainly on the impact of restorative justice on offenders. Indeed, the systematic observation of conferencing used in the quantitative analysis explicitly focuses on observations of the offender. While we do not yet know the effects of an interaction ritual for victims of crime, the video analysis suggests that victims also benefit, displaying signs of solidarity and emotional energy following a conference. This suggests that future research might include both systematic observations of victims and qualitative interviews exploring their long-term emotional states.

Restorative justice theory and practice can also benefit from more data collected with an explicit interaction ritual focus. My qualitative research was designed to explore elements of interaction ritual theory in restorative justice and so the interview questions, as well as the coding criteria for the video, were developed with this in mind. As a result, I provide a rich examination of interaction ritual in restorative justice. The quantitative data was collected with a different focus and different goals as the RISE researchers were not looking to test interaction ritual theory. I have used the systematic observations to approximate interaction ritual ingredients and outcomes as best I could. Future research will include systematic observations of conferences where observers are trained to pick up on the micro interactional cues to measure concepts such as rhythm, balance, solidarity, and emotional energy. In order to achieve this, we need to develop consistent micro measures for rhythm and balance. Research design that is focused on capturing these micro sociological variables will offer stronger tests of interaction ritual theory in restorative justice conferences.

In addition to reoffending, evaluating participants' long-term emotional energy levels will provide us with further refinement of the theory of restorative justice. This can be obtained through a series of in-depth interviews with offenders, participants, and supporters (and facilitators, as they too benefit emotionally from participation in restorative justice). Tracking emotional energy over time can give us a sense of how long it takes for emotional energy to decay, as well as the influence of other interaction rituals in a person's life.

Recommendations for Best Practice

Facilitators have an implicit understanding of what it takes to create a powerful conference and many already use effective strategies to manage emotions and develop solidarity. This can be made even more explicit with training. My interviews and observations strongly convince me that the best way to encourage successful restorative justice conferences is through the proper training of effective facilitators. A presentation of interaction ritual theory and evidence can teach facilitators the value of encouraging emotional build-up; arranging a suitable and safe space; and developing rhythm and balance. Facilitators can be trained in Ekman's facial coding scheme (Ekman and Friesen, 1975; Ekman and Rosenberg, 1998) so they have an idea of what emotions participants are feeling. In training they can deconstruct conference videos as was achieved in Chapter Four, by pausing, rewinding, and slowing down interaction to see exactly how rhythm develops. They can also engage in positive interaction ritual so they too can experience solidarity and emotional energy. As I went through facilitator training with the police officers, we participated in a number of mock conferences, with each of us taking turns playing the roles of offender, victim, supporter, and facilitator. Amazingly, even though we were role-playing, we really did begin to develop solidarity and feelings of emotional energy through the conference. We took on the roles assigned and began to feel the actual emotions and entrainment required for successful interaction. This experience was quite instructive, helping us to become keenly sensitive to the micro dynamics of a conference. Incorporating an awareness of the micro dynamics of interaction rituals and strategies to encourage ritual success can improve the effectiveness of conferencing.

Based on the findings presented in this book, I will provide some practical recommendations for restorative justice practitioners and researchers who want to maximize emotions and interactional dynamics to encourage ritual success. A facilitator cannot guarantee that a conference will have an emotional turning point, or that it will result in solidarity, reintegration, and emotional energy. The best they can do is to ensure that the ritual ingredients are present so that the likelihood of ritual success is increased. I present here a checklist of requirements for a successful interaction.

1. In meetings with conference participants prior to the conference, encourage a frank discussion of the effects of the crime and emotions. This will begin the build-up needed for emotional intensity.
2. Ensure adequate space and privacy. Have a clean room with the chairs arranged in a circle in advance of the conference. Put thought into the seating arrangement, with strategic placement of 'buffers' to minimize conflict.
3. Restorative justice conferences should be face-to-face meetings. Shuttle mediation will not effectively entrain the participants into the rhythm of the interaction.
4. Ensure supporters are present for both victim and offender.
5. Use different strategies to encourage rhythmic entrainment. Let embarrassing silences continue since a participant will jump in to fill a gap and encourage conversation. Encourage direct eye contact between victim and offender.
6. Prevent and lessen perceived imbalances. Be sensitive to the power and status dynamics developing between participants.
7. Encourage the development of strong collective symbols to represent the interaction.
8. Encourage touching. While one does not want to force physical interaction, touching between participants is one strategy to encourage positive emotions. For instance, a facilitator can encourage a handshake between victim and offender at the conclusion of a conference.
9. If successful, repeat interaction. Hold follow-up conferences to recharge participants with emotional energy.

These suggestions are informed by theory and research on the micro dynamics of restorative justice. My research has shown what makes restorative justice 'work' to bring people together to transform a victim-offender relationship from one of conflict to one of solidarity. This perspective can improve restorative justice theory and practice. While a successful conference may provide emotional transformation on a micro scale, the success of restorative justice as a social movement may lead to the transformation of criminal justice for all.

Appendix 1
Qualitative Interview Guide

(Note: These questions were used as a guide to semi-structure the interviews. They were guidelines to explore the different themes in the conference.)

Offender Consent

a. Describe the offender.
b. Do you remember your initial meeting with Describe.
c. Where did you meet with them.
d. What were your impressions of the offender at the time of the first interview?
e. How long did you meet for?
f. What did you talk about?
g. What were this person's thoughts about the meetings? (If thoughts were not positive, then how did you convince them?)
h. What were your feelings coming out of the initial meeting?
i. How did you think the conference would go? What were your reasons for this hypothesis?

Offender Supporter Consent

a. Can you tell me about each meeting you had with the offender supporter(s)?
b. Did they all know each other? Did you meet as a group initially?
c. What were this person's thoughts about the meetings? (If thoughts were not positive, then how did you convince them?)
d. Were there any other potential offender supporters that you would have liked to have been there that you were unable to get there? Who and why?
e. Were there any offender supporters there that you felt should not have been there? Who and why?

Victim Consent

a. How many victims were there in this case? Describe.
b. Were there other victims that did not want to take part?
c. Do you remember your initial meeting with them?

d. Where did you meet?
e. How long did you meet for?
f. What did you talk about?
g. How did you convince them to participate?
h. What were your feelings coming out of the meeting?
i. Did you think it would be a good conference? Why or why not?
j. What were your impressions of the victim at the time of the first interview?

Victim Supporter Consent

a. Can you tell me about each meeting you had with the victim supporter (s)?
b. Did they all know each other? Did you meet as a group initially?
c. How did you convince them to participate?
d. Were there any other potential victim supporters that you would have liked to have been there that you were unable to get there? Who and why?
e. Was there anybody there that you felt should not have been there? Who and why?

Observers

a. Were there any outside observers for the conference? Who?
b. Did you feel that having the observers there affected the conference in any way? How?
c. Did any of the observers have any contact with conference participants? What kind?

Location

a. Where was the conference held (prison/bail)?
b. Can you describe the conference room? Was it private? Was it a suitable room?
c. What set-up was involved?
d. Was the room arranged in a circle? Was there a table in the centre? [Refer to map in files.] Who was sitting next to whom? Was that on purpose? Why did you arrange it like that?
e. [In prison] Did you have any problems getting into the prison? Were there any long waits? Were the victims and supporters searched?
f. How did everybody get to the location? Did they drive themselves? Did you drive? Was anybody late? How late was the conference?
g. How long did you have the room booked for? Was that enough time? Were you asked to leave early?
h. Were you satisfied with the conference room? Why or why not? How could it have been better?

Pre-Conference

a. Did you travel with the victim to the conference? Can you assess how they felt? Were they nervous or embarrassed? [Ask same question for offender and supporters.]

b. Were you with the victim right before the conference? Can you assess how they felt? Were they nervous or embarrassed? [Ask same question for offender and supporters.]

At the Conference: Shared Mood/Rhythm

a. During the conference: Did you think the offender was nervous? How did they show this?

b. Did you think they were embarrassed? How did they show this? [Ask same questions for victim and supporters.]

c. Did you think they were angry? How did they show this? [Ask same questions for victim and supporters.]

d. What other emotions do you think the conference participants were feeling?

e. What were you feeling?

f. Were the participants willing to talk from the beginning? Who was first to speak? Did you follow the conference script?

g. Were there long silences? Did they make you uncomfortable? How do you think conference participants reacted to the silences?

h. Did you use the silences like we were taught in training?

i. Did the gaps and silences eventually lessen or stop? At what point did that happen? Can you remember for how many seconds there was silence? What was the longest pause? How many gaps were there?

j. Did you notice a rhythm develop during the conference?

k. Was there a moment when the conversation 'took off'? At what point did that happen?

l. Was there any point during the conference when people were speaking at once? How long a gap was there between one person finishing speaking and the next person starting? Did you feel that you needed to intervene to keep the conversation going smoothly?

m. Was there any yelling during the conference or raised voices? Were people speaking at once? How did that come about? How did you deal with that?

n. Did you think that the victim and offender had equal amounts of time to speak? Did one speak more than the other?

o. Role of supporters: Were offender supporters supportive or condemning of the offender: How do you think the supporters helped/harmed the conference?

p. Do you remember how the participants were sitting during the conference? How was the room arranged? Who was sitting next to whom?

   i. How was the offender sitting (posture)?

    ii. How was the victim sitting (posture)?

    iii. Were the offender and offender supporters touching? What about the victim and victim supporters?

Mutual Focus of Attention

a. Did the offender pay attention to what the victim was saying? Did you have to intervene at all?

b. Did the victim pay attention to what the offender was saying? Did you have to intervene at all?

c. Did all the participants pay attention to what you were saying?

d. Were there any shared symbolic gestures?

Empathy/Symbols of Interaction

a. Were there any moments of empathy? Did they see each other's point of view? Can you describe how this came about?

b. Did the offender and victim know each other's names? Did they call each other by name? Did the victim use a pseudonym?

c. During the course of the conference did the offender and victim realize anything that they had in common (for example, drink at the same pub, live in the same neighbourhood, fans of the same football club)? Do you remember how this came about? How did they react when they realized this?

d. Did you have a chance to speak to the offender or the victim after the conference? How do you think they felt? Were they satisfied with the conference? Were they proud of their participation? Were they more or less angry?

e. Did you feel that you had a good relationship with the offender? Do you think they liked you? Do you feel that they respected you?

f. Did you feel that you had a good relationship with the victim? Do you think they liked you? Do you feel that they respected you?

Outcome Agreement ('OA')

a. What do you remember about the discussion around the OA?

b. Did the victims want something that offenders didn't agree to, or vice versa?

c. Was it all signed and did they all get copies?

d. Was there any follow-up on the OA? How did you follow up on each item? What were the results? [Go through each OA item from the case file].

e. How useful do you think outcome agreements are? Do you think that offenders and victims take them seriously? Do you think they respect them?

f. Did you think the offender felt they were being punished? Did they think this was fair?

Group Solidarity

a. Do you remember if the offender and victim, or any of the other participants, shook hands at any point during the conference? Who and when?

b. Did anybody hug each other or pat each other on the back? Who and when?

c. Can you remember any moments when people laughed together? Can you remember how it came about?

d. Did anybody cry during the conference? Who was crying and at what point? What was the reaction to the crying?

e. Was eye contact made during the conference? Do you remember using the click and drag approach successfully (when facilitators lock eyes with one person and consciously drag their vision to another person to encourage eye contact between two people)?

f. Did the participants seem animated or excited when they were talking to each other? Was this level of excitement the same through all of the conference, or did it change?

g. After the conference, was there a 'tea and biscuits' phase, where offender and victim informally interacted while you were writing up the outcome agreement?
   i. Did you witness it?
   ii. Did they seem comfortable with each other?
   iii. Can you remember what they spoke about?
   iv. Did you think this was a significant part of the conference?

Conference Rating

a. Right after the conference, you gave it a rating of ____ out of ten. Do you remember this?

b. Can you remember why you gave it that rating?

c. You may have also been asked if there was a 'cathartic moment' during the conference. At that time you said it was when _____.
   Do you remember that? Can you describe that more in-depth to me?

d. In your judgment, how emotional was the conference?

e. Did you feel emotionally affected by the conference?

f. Looking back, would you still rate it a ____? Can you explain why?

g. In terms of facilitation, was this an easy or hard conference to facilitate? Can you explain how?

h. Do you think that this offender will reoffend?

Appendix 2
Qualitative Coding Key for
Interaction Ritual

Face-to-face:	offender and victim talking face-to-face in the same room
Privacy:	facilitator assessment of outside interruptions to the conference
Rhythm:	facilitator describes the conference as having 'flow', or specifying a rhythm developing over time
Space adequacy:	problems identified with the room, noise, temperature, size, lighting, uncomfortable
Balance:	equal contribution by all parties at the conference. Facilitator notes that if one party dominates the other, this disrupts the 'flow'
Turning point:	facilitator identifies and describes in detail one or more specific points of the conference they see as an emotional high point
Supporters:	supporters for each party present at the conference
Touching:	hugging, shoulder rubbing, handshake, pats on back
Eye contact:	facilitator assessment of eye contact or avoidance of eye contact during the conference
Apology:	apology explicitly made
Apology accepted:	apology explicitly accepted/forgiveness offered
Crying:	any participant crying at any point during the conference
Smiling:	any participants smiling at each other at any point during the conference
Laughing:	laughter between parties

Appendix 3
Ekman's Facial Coding Scheme
(Source: Ekman and Friesen, 1975)

Surprise

- The brows are raised, so that they are curved and high.
- The skin below the brow is stretched.
- Horizontal wrinkles across the forehead.
- The eyelids are opened; the upper lid is raised and the lower lid drawn down; the whites of the eyes show above the iris and often below as well.
- The jaw drops open so that the lips and teeth are parted, but there is no tension or stretching of the mouth.

Fear

- The brows are raised and drawn together.
- The wrinkles in the forehead are in the centre, not across the entire forehead.
- The upper eyelid is raised, exposing the whites of the eyes, and the lower eyelid is tensed and drawn up.
- The mouth is open and the lips are either tensed slightly and drawn back or stretched and drawn back.

Disgust

- The upper lip is raised.
- The lower lip is also raised and pushed up to the upper lip, or is lowered and slightly protruding.
- The nose is wrinkled.
- The cheeks are raised.
- Lines show below the lower lid, and the lid is pushed up but not tense.
- The brow is lowered, lowering the upper lid.

Anger

- The brows are lowered and drawn together.
- Vertical lines appear between the brows.
- The lower lid is tense and may or may not be raised.
- The upper lid is tense and may or may not be lowered by the action of the brow.
- The eyes have a hard stare and may have a bulging appearance.

- The lips are in either of two basic positions: pressed firmly together, with the corners straight down; or open, tensed in a squarish shape as if shouting.
- The nostrils may be dilated, but not essential to anger (also occurs in sadness).
- There are ambiguities unless anger is registered in all three facial areas.

Happiness

- The corners of the lips are drawn back and up.
- The mouth may or may not be parted, with teeth exposed or not.
- A wrinkle runs down from the nose to the outer edge beyond the lip corners.
- The cheeks are raised.
- The lower eyelids show wrinkles, and may be raised but not tense.
- Crow's feet wrinkles go outwards from the outer corners of the eyes.

Sadness

- The inner corners of the eyebrow are drawn up.
- The skin below the eyebrow is triangulated, with the inner corner up.
- The upper eyelid inner corner is raised.
- The corners of the lips are down or the lip is trembling.

Appendix 4
Key Questions from the RISE Observation Instrument

Conference observers completed this instrument using eight-point scales:

1. How much support was the offender given during the conference?
2. How much reintegrative shaming was expressed?
3. How reintegrative was the conference for this offender?
4. How much approval of the offender as a person was expressed?
5. How much was the offender treated by their supporters as someone they love?
6. How much respect for the offender was expressed?
7. How much disapproval of the offender's act was expressed?
8. How much stigmatizing shaming was expressed?
9. How much disappointment in the offender was expressed?
10. To what extent was the offender treated as a criminal?
11. How often were stigmatizing names and labels (eg, 'criminal', 'punk', 'junkie', or 'bully') used to describe the offender?
12. How much moral indignation did the victim party(s) express about the offender's actions?
13. How much disapproval of the offender as a person was expressed?
14. To what extent did the offender accept that they had done wrong?
15. How sorry/remorseful was the offender for their actions?
16. When reaching the conference outcome, how severe was the offender on themselves?
17. Did the offender apologize? (yes/no)
18. If the offender apologized, what form did the apology take? (state number of times each type was expressed: verbal, handshake, hug, pat on shoulder, kiss, other)
19. To what extent was the offender forgiven for their actions?
20. How clearly was it communicated to the offender that they could put their actions behind them?
21. How much forgiveness of the offender was expressed?
22. If the offender was forgiven, what form did the forgiveness take? (state number of times each type was expressed: verbal, handshake, hug, pat on shoulder, kiss, other)
23. How much did the offender claim their actions were accidental or unintentional?

24. To what extent did the offender hold others responsible for their actions?
25. How defiant (ie, cocky, bold, brashly confident) was the offender?
26. How sullen/unresponsive was the offender?
27. How emotionally powerful was the account given of the consequences of the offender's act?
28. How emotionally responsive was the offender to the account given of the consequences of their act?
29. How much discussion of the consequences of the offender's actions occurred?
30. How much discussion of the consequences (even if not realized) of this type of offence occurred?
31. How much did the offender contribute to the conference outcome?
32. How much was the offender coerced into accepting the conference outcome?
33. How much responsibility did the offender take for their actions?
34. How much did the offender retreat from, and avoid the attention of, others?
35. How much was the offender's speech affected by irregularities, pauses, or incoherence?
36. How uncomfortable (eg, restless, anxious, fidgety) was the offender?
37. To what extent did the offender engage in hiding (eg, lowering head) and concealing (eg, hand covering parts of face, averting gaze) behaviour?
38. What percentage of the conference time was taken up by the offender talking?
39. How much did the offender contribute to the conference?
40. How much was the offender dominated?
41. How much moral lecturing was directed at the offender?
42. How clearly were the possible consequences of future offences communicated to the offender?
43. If the possible consequences of future offences were communicated to the offender, to what extent was this done in a non-threatening or matter-of-fact way?
44. How much was the offender harassed?
45. How often was the offender shouted at?
46. Overall, how emotionally engaged was the offender?
47. How much approval of the offender's criminal actions was expressed?
48. At any stage of the conference, did the offender cry? (yes/no)
49. Was an outcome relating to this offender reached at the conference? (yes/no)
50. How much consensus was there among conference participants about the conference outcome for this offender?

References

Ahmed, E., N. Harris, J. Braithwaite, and V. Braithwaite (2001) *Shame Management Through Reintegration,* Cambridge: Cambridge University Press.

Angel, C. (2005) 'Crime Victims Meet Their Offenders: Testing the Impact of Restorative Justice Conferences on Victims' Post-Traumatic Stress Symptoms', PhD Dissertation, Department of Criminology, University of Pennsylvania.

Arendt, H. (1963) *Eichmann in Jerusalem: A Report on the Banality of Evil,* New York: Penguin Books.

Atkinson, J. M. and J. Heritage (1984) *Structures of Social Action: Studies in Conversation Analysis,* Cambridge: Cambridge University Press.

Barnes, G. C. (1999) 'Procedural Justice in Two Contexts: Testing the Fairness of Diversionary Conferencing for Intoxicated Drivers', PhD Dissertation: Department of Criminology, University of Maryland.

Bennett, C. (2008) *The Apology Ritual: A Philosophical Theory of Punishment,* Cambridge: Cambridge University Press.

Bilchik, S. (1998) 'Guide for Implementing the Balanced and Restorative Justice Model', Office of Justice Programs, Bureau of Justice Assistance, US Department of Justice.

Bradshaw, W. and D. Roseborough (2005) 'Restorative Justice Dialogue: The Impact of Mediation and Conferencing on Juvenile Recidivism', *Federal Probation,* 69/2: 1521.

Braithwaite, J. (1989) *Crime, Shame and Reintegration,* Cambridge: Cambridge University Press.

Braithwaite, J. (2000) 'Survey Article: Repentance Rituals and Restorative Justice', *Journal of Political Philosophy,* 8/1: 115–31.

Braithwaite, J. (2002) *Restorative Justice and Responsive Regulation,* Oxford: Oxford University Press.

Braithwaite, J. (2006) 'Compulsory Compassion: A Critique of Restorative Justice', *Law and Social Inquiry Journal of the American Bar Foundation,* 31/2: 423–44.

Braithwaite, J., A. Ahmed, and V. Braithwaite (2006) 'Shame, Restorative Justice, and Crime' in F. Cullen, J. Wright, and K. Blevins (eds) *Taking Stock: The Status of Criminological Theory (Advances in Criminological Theory),* 15: 397–417. Transaction Publishers.

Braithwaite, J. and V. Braithwaite (2001) 'Part I. Shame, Shame Management and Regulation' in E. Ahmed, N. Harris, J. Braithwaite, and V. Braithwaite (eds) *Shame Management Through Reintegration,* Cambridge: Cambridge University Press: 3–72.

Braithwaite, J. and S. Mugford (1994), 'Conditions of Successful Reintegration Ceremonies: Dealing with Juvenile Offenders', *British Journal of Criminology*, 34/2: 139–171.

Choi, J. J., G. Bazemore, and M. J. Gilbert (2012) 'Review of Research on Victims' Experiences in Restorative Justice: Implications for Youth Justice', *Children and Youth Services Review*, 34/1: 35–42.

Coates, R. B. and J. Gehm (1989) 'An Empirical Assessment' in M. Wright and B. Galaway (eds) *Mediation and Criminal Justice*, London: Sage, 251–263.

Collins, R. (1990) 'Stratification, Emotional Energy, and Transient Emotions' in T. D. Kemper (ed) *Research Agendas in the Sociology of Emotions*, Albany: SUNY Press: 27–57.

Collins, R. (1993) 'Emotional Energy as the Common Denominator of Rational Action', *Rationality and Society*, 5/2: 203.

Collins, R. (2004) *Interaction Ritual Chains*, Princeton: Princeton University Press.

Cook, K. J. (2006) 'Doing Difference and Accountability in Restorative Justice Conferences', *Theoretical Criminology*, 10/1: 107–124.

Daly, K. (2001) 'Restorative Justice: The Real Story', *Punishment and Society*, 4: 55–79.

Daly, K. and J. Stubbs (2006) 'Feminist Engagement with Restorative Justice', *Theoretical Criminology*, 10/1: 9–28.

De Beus, K. and N. Rodriguez (2007) 'Restorative Justice Practice: An Examination of Program Completion and Recidivism', *Journal of Criminal Justice*, 35/3: 337–47.

Doak, J. and D. O'Mahony (2011) 'In Search of Legitimacy: Restorative Youth Conferencing in Northern Ireland', *Legal Studies*, 31/2: 305–25.

Durkheim, E. (1912) *Elementary Forms of Religious Life*, New York: The Free Press.

Ekman, P. (2001) *Telling Lies: Clues to Deceit in the Marketplace, Politics, and Marriage*, New York: Norton.

Ekman, P. and W. Friesen (1975) *Unmasking the Face: A Guide to Recognizing Emotions from Facial Cues*, Englewood Cliffs: Prentice Hall.

Ekman, P. and E. L. Rosenberg (1998) *What the Face Reveals: Basic and Applied Studies of Spontaneous Expression*, Oxford: Oxford University Press.

Evje, A. and R. C. Cushman, (2000) 'A Summary of the Evaluations of Six California Victim Offender Reconciliation Programs', The Judicial Council of California, Administrative Office of the Courts.

Foucault, M. (1977) *Discipline and Punishment*, New York: Pantheon.

Garfinkel, H. (1967) *Studies in Ethnomethodology*, NJ: Englewood Cliffs.

Garland, D. (1993) *Punishment and Modern Society: A Study in Social Theory*, Chicago: University of Chicago Press.

Goffman, E. (1959) *The Presentation of Self in Everyday Life*, New York: Doubleday.

Goffman, E. (1961) *Encounters: Two Studies in the Sociology of Interaction*, Indianapolis: Bobbs-Merrill Company.

Goffman, E. (1967) *Interaction Ritual*, New York: Doubleday.

Goffman, E. (1981) *Forms of Talk*, Oxford: Blackwell.

Grindstaff, L. (2002) *The Money Shot: Trash, Class, and the Making of TV Talk Shows*, Chicago: University of Chicago Press.

Harris, N. (2001) 'Shaming and Shame: Regulating Drink-Driving' in E. Ahmed, N. Harris, J. Braithwaite, and V. Braithwaite (eds) *Shame Management Through Reintegration*, Cambridge: Cambridge University Press: 73–210.

Harris, N. (2003) 'Reassessing the Dimensionality of the Moral Emotions', *British Journal of Psychology*, 94: 457–73.

Harris, N. and J. B. Burton (1998) 'Testing the Reliability of Observational Measures of Reintegrative Shaming at Community Accountability Conferences and at Court', *Australian and New Zealand Journal of Criminology*, 31/3: 230.

Harris, N. and S. Maruna (2006) 'Shame, Shaming and Restorative Justice' in D. Sullivan and L. Tiff (eds) *Handbook of Restorative Justice*, Abingdon: Routledge: 452–62.

Harris, N., L. Walgrave, and J. Braithwaite (2004) 'Emotional Dynamics in Restorative Conferences', *Theoretical Criminology*, 8/2: 191–210.

Hayes, H. and K. Daly (2003) 'Youth Justice Conferencing and Reoffending', *Justice Quarterly*, 20/4: 725–64.

Hayes, H. and K. Daly (2004) 'Conferencing and Re-offending in Queensland', *Australian and New Zealand Journal of Criminology*, 37/2: 167–91.

Hochschild, A. R. (1983) *The Managed Heart: Commercialization of Human Feeling*, Berkeley: University of California Press.

Home Office (2003) 'Restorative Justice: The Government's Strategy', The Home Office.

Hoyle, C., R. Young, and R. Hill (2002) *Proceed with Caution: An Evaluation of the Thames Valley Police Initiative in Restorative Cautioning*, York: Joseph Rowntree Foundation.

Hughes, P. and M. J. Mossman (2001) 'Re-Thinking Access to Criminal Justice in Canada: A Critical Review of Needs, Responses and Restorative Justice Initiatives', Research and Statistics Division, Department of Justice, Canada.

Immarigeon, R. and K. Daly (1997) 'Restorative Justice: Origins, Practices, Contexts, and Challenges', *The ICCA Journal on Community Corrections*, 8/2: 13–19.

Jones, C. (2009) 'Does Forum Sentencing Reduce Re-Offending?' New South Wales Bureau of Crime Statistics and Research.

Karstedt, S. (2002) 'Emotions and Criminal Justice', *Theoretical Criminology*, 6/3: 299–317.

Karstedt, S. (2006) 'Emotions, Crime, and Justice: Exploring Durkheimian Themes' in M. Deflem (ed) *Sociological Theory and Criminological Research: Views from Europe and the United States*, Oxford: Elsevier: 223–48.

Katz, J. (1988) *Seductions of Crime: Moral and Sensual Attractions in Doing Evil*, Arizona: Basic Books.

Katz, J. (2001) *How Emotions Work*, Chicago: University of Chicago Press.

King, M. S. (2008) 'Restorative Justice, Therapeutic Jurisprudence and the Rise of Emotionally Intelligent Justice', *Melbourne University Law Review*, 32/3: 1096–126.

Lambert, D. (1992) 'Zero-inflated Poisson Regression, with an Application to Defects in Manufacturing', *Technometrics*, 34(1): 1–14.

Latimer, J., C. Dowden, and D. Muise (2005), 'The Effectiveness of Restorative Justice Practices: A Meta-analysis', *Prison Journal*, 85/2: 127–44.

Laub, J. and R. Sampson (2003) *Shared Beginnings, Divergent Lives: Delinquent Boys to Age Seventy*, Cambridge: Harvard University Press.

Lee, A. (1996) 'Public Attitudes Towards Restorative Justice' in B. Galaway and J. Hudson (eds) *Restorative Justice: International Perspectives*, Montsey: Criminal Justice Press.

Long, J. S. and J. Freese (2006) *Regression Models for Categorical Dependent Variables using STATA*, College Station, TX: Stata Press.

Luke, G. and B. Lind (2002) 'Reducing Juvenile Crime: Conferencing versus Court', New South Wales Bureau of Crime Statistics and Research.

Macaulay, R. (2006) 'The Social Art: Language and Its Uses' Oxford: Oxford University Press.

Marshall, T. (1999) 'Restorative Justice: An Overview', London: Home Office Research Development and Statistics Directorate.

Maruna, S. (2001) *Making Good: How Ex-Convicts Reform and Rebuild Their Lives*, Washington, DC: American Psychological Association.

Maruna, S. (2011) 'Reentry as a Rite of Passage', *Punishment and Society*, 13/1: 3–28.

Maxwell, G., and A. Morris (2001) 'Family group conferences and reoffending *Restorative Justice for Juveniles. Conferencing, Mediation and Circles*', Oxford and Portland: Hart Publishing: 243–63.

Maynard, D. W. and J. F. Manzo (1993) 'On the Sociology of Justice: Theoretical Notes From an Actual Jury Deliberation' *Sociological Theory*, 11/2: 171.

McCold, P. and B. Wachtel (1998) *Restorative Policing Experiment: The Bethlehem Pennsylvania Police Family Group Conferencing Project*, Pipersville, PA: Community Service Foundation.

McGarrell, E. F. (2000) *Returning Justice to the Community: The Indianapolis Juvenile Restorative Justice Experiment*, Indianapolis: Hudson Institute.

McGarrell, E. F. and N. K. Hipple (2007) 'Family Group Conferencing and Re-offending Among First-Time Juvenile Offenders: The Indianapolis Experiment', *Justice Quarterly*, 24/2: 221–46.

Morris, A. and G. M. Maxwell (1993) 'Juvenile Justice in New Zealand: A New Paradigm', *Australian and New Zealand Journal of Criminology,* 26/1: 72–90.

Morris, A. and G. M. Maxwell (1998) 'Restorative Justice in New Zealand: Family Group Conferences as a Case Study', *Western Criminology Review,* 1/1: 1–18.

Morris, A., G. M. Maxwell, and J. P. Robertson (1993) 'Giving Victims a Voice: A New Zealand Experiment', *The Howard Journal of Criminal Justice,* 32/4: 304–21.

New Zealand Ministry of Justice and Strategic Assessment Group (2004) 'Restorative Justice in New Zealand: Best Practice', Wellington: New Zealand Ministry of Justice.

Nugent, W. R., M. Williams, and M. S. Umbreit (2004) 'Participation in Victim-Offender Mediation and the Prevalence of Subsequent Delinquent Behavior: A Meta-Analysis', *Research on Social Work Practice,* 14/6: 408–16.

Pfohl, S. J. (1981) 'Labelling Criminals' in H. L. Ross (ed) *Law and Deviance,* Beverly Hills: Sage.

Poulson, B. (2003) 'Third Voice: A Review of Empirical Research on the Psychological Outcomes of Restorative Justice', *Utah Law Review,* 2003/1: 167–203.

Pranis, K. and M. Umbreit (1992) *Public Opinion Research Challenges Perception of Widespread Public Demand for Harsher Punishment,* Minneapolis, MN: Citizens Council.

Pratt, J. (1996) 'Colonization, Power and Silence: A History of Indigenous Justice in New Zealand Society' in B. Galaway and J. Hudson (eds) *Restorative Justice: International Perspectives,* Montsey: Criminal Justice Press: 137–56.

Retzinger, S. and T. Scheff (1996) 'Strategy for Community Conferences: Emotions and Social Bonds' in B. Galaway and J. Hudson (eds) *Restorative Justice: International Perspectives,* Montsey: Criminal Justice Press: 315–36.

Robinson, G. and J. Shapland (2008) 'Reducing Recidivism: A Task for Restorative Justice?', *British Journal of Criminology,* 48/3: 337–58.

Rodriguez, N. (2007) 'Restorative Justice at Work: Examining the Impact of Restorative Justice Resolutions on Juvenile Recidivism', *Crime and Delinquency,* 53/3: 355–79.

Rossner, M. (2011) 'Emotions and Interaction Ritual: A Micro Analysis of Restorative Justice', *British Journal of Criminology,* 51/1: 95.

Sacks, H., E. A. Schegloff, and G. Jefferson (1974) 'A Simplest Systematics for the Organization of Turn-Taking for Conversation', *Language,* 4/1: 696–735.

Schechner, R. (1981) 'Performers and Spectators Transported and Transformed', *The Kenyon Review,* 3/4: 83–113.

Scheff, T. J. (1990) *Microsociology: Discourse, Emotion, and Social Structure,* Chicago: University of Chicago Press.

Scheff, T. J. and S. M. Retzinger (1991) *Emotions and Violence: Shame and Rage in Destructive Conflicts,* Lexington: Lexington Books.

Schneider, A. L. (1986) 'Restitution and Recidivism Rates of Juvenile Offenders: Results from Four Experimental Studies', *Criminology,* 24/3: 533–52.

Seligman, M. E. P. (2002), *Authentic Happiness: Using the New Positive Psychology to Realize Your Potential for Lasting Fulfillment,* New York: Free Press.

Shapland, J., A. Atkinson, H. Atkinson, B. Chapman, J. Dignan, M. Howes, J. Johnstone, G. Robinson, and A. Sorsby (2007) 'Restorative Justice: the Views of Victims and Offenders', *Ministry of Justice Research Series,* 3/07.

Shapland, J., A. Atkinson, H. Atkinson, E. Colledge, J. Dignan, M. Howes, J. Johnstone, G. Robinson, and A. Sorsby (2006) 'Situating Restorative Justice within Criminal Justice', *Theoretical Criminology,* 10/4: 505–32.

Shapland, J., A. Atkinson, H. Atkinson, J. Dignan, L. Edwards, J. Hibbert, M. Howes, J. Johnstone, G. Robinson, and A. Sorsby (2008) 'Does Restorative Justice Affect Reconviction?: The Fourth Report From the Evaluation of Three Schemes', *Ministry of Justice Research Series,* 10/08.

Shapland, J., A. Atkinson, E. Colledge, J. Dignan, M. Howes, J. Johnstone, R. Pennant, G. Robinson, and A. Sorsby (2004) 'Implementing Restorative Justice Schemes (Crime Reduction Programme): A Report on the First Year', *Home Office Online Report,* 32/04.

Shaw, C. R. (1966) *The Jack-Roller: A Delinquent Boy's Own Story,* Chicago: University of Chicago Press.

Sherman, L. W. (1993) 'Defiance, Deterrence, and Irrelevance: A Theory of the Criminal Sanction', *Journal of Research in Crime and Delinquency,* 30/4: 445–73.

Sherman, L. W. (2003) 'Reason for Emotion: Reinventing Justice with Theories, Innovations, and Research—The American Society of Criminology 2002 Presidential Address', *Criminology,* 41/1: 1–37.

Sherman, L. W. and G. C. Barnes (1997) 'Restorative Justice and Offenders' Respect for the Law', Reintegrative Shaming Experiment (RISE) Working Paper No 3, Australian National University.

Sherman, L. W. and H. Strang (2007), *Restorative Justice: The Evidence,* London: The Smith Institute.

Sherman, L. W. and H. Strang (2011) 'Empathy for the Devil' in S. Karstedt, I. Loader, and H. Strang (eds) *Emotions, Crime and Justice,* Oxford: Hart Publishing.

Sherman, L. W. and H. Strang (2012) 'Restorative Justice and Evidence-Based Sentencing' in J. Petersilia and K. Reitz (eds) *The Oxford Handbook of Sentencing and Corrections,* Oxford: Oxford University Press: 215–45.

Sherman, L. W., H. Strang, G. C. Barnes, J. Braithwaite, N. Inkpen, and M. Teh (1998) 'Experiments in Restorative Policing: A Progress Report to the National Police Research Unit on the Canberra Reintegrative Shaming Experiments (RISE)', Canberra: Australian National University.

Sherman, L. W., H. Strang, C. Angel, M. Rossner, D. Woods, G. C. Barnes, S. Bennett, and N. Inkpen (2005) 'Effects of Face-to-Face Restorative Justice on Victims of Crime in Four Randomized, Controlled Trials', *Journal of Experimental Criminology*, 1/3: 367–95.

Sherman, L. W., H. Strang, and D. Woods (2000) 'Recidivism Patterns in the Canberra Reintegrative Shaming Experiments', Canberra: Australian National University.

Sherman, L. W., H. Strang, and D. Woods (2004) 'Restorative Justice Effects on Repeat Offending After Violent and Property Crimes: Differential Effects in Two Randomized Trials', Paper presented at the Meetings of the American Society of Criminology.

Strang, H. (2002) *Repair or Revenge: Victims and Restorative Justice*, Oxford: Oxford University Press.

Strang, H. and L. W. Sherman (1997) 'The Victim's Perspective', Reintegrative Shaming Experiment (RISE) Working Paper No 2, Australian National University.

Strang, H. and L. W. Sherman (2004) 'Protocol for a Campbell Collaboration Systematic Review: Effects of Face-to-Face Restorative Justice for Personal Victim Crimes', Campbell Crime and Justice Group.

Tangney, J. P. (1995) 'Recent Advances in the Empirical Study of Shame and Guilt', *American Behavioral Scientist*, 38/8: 1132–45.

Taylor Griffiths, C. and R. Hamilton (1996) 'Sanctioning and Healings: Restorative Justice in Canadian Aboriginal Communities' in B. Galaway and J. Hudson (eds) *Restorative Justice: International Perspectives*, Montsey: Criminal Justice Press: 175–92.

Tkachuk, B. (2002) *Criminal Justice Reform: Lessons Learned: Community Involvement and Restorative Justice,* European Institute for Crime Prevention and Control, Helsinki.

Triggs, S. (2005) *New Zealand Court-Referred Restorative Justice Pilot: Two Year Follow-Up of Reoffending,* Wellington: New Zealand Ministry of Justice.

Turner, J. (2000) *On the Origin of Human Emotion*, Stanford, CA: Stanford University Press.

Tyler, T. R. (1990) *Why People Obey the Law: Procedural Justice, Legitimacy, and Compliance*, New Haven: Yale University Press.

Tyler, T. R., P. Degoey, and H. Smith (1996) 'Understanding Why the Justice of Group Procedures Matters: A Test of the Psychological Dynamics of the Group-Value Model', *Journal of Personality and Social Psychology*, 70: 913–31.

Tyler, T. R. and Y. J. Huo (2002) *Trust in the Law: Encouraging Public Cooperation with the Police and Courts,* New York: Russell Sage Foundation Publications.

Tyler, T. R., L. W. Sherman, H. Strang, G. C. Barnes, and D. Woods (2007) 'Reintegrative Shaming, Procedural Justice, and Recidivism: The Engagement of Offenders' Psychological Mechanisms in the Canberra RISE Drinking-and-Driving Experiment', *Law and Society Review,* 41/3: 553–85.

Umbreit, M. (1998) 'Restorative Justice Through Victim-Offender Mediation: A Multisite Assessment', *Western Criminology Review,* 1/1: 1–29.

Umbreit, M. S. and R. B. Coates (1993) 'Cross-Site Analysis of Victim-Offender Mediation in Four States', *Crime and Delinquency,* 39/4: 565–85.

Umbreit, M., R. B. Coates, and B. Kalanj (1994) *Victim Meets Offender: The Impact of Restorative Justice and Mediation,* New York: Criminal Justice Press.

Umbreit, M., R. B. Coates, and A. Roberts (2000) 'The Impact of Victim-Offender Mediation: A Cross-National Perspective', *Mediation Quarterly,* 17/3: 215–29.

Van Stokkom, B. (2002) 'Moral Emotions in Restorative Justice Conferences: Managing Shame, Designing Empathy', *Theoretical Criminology,* 6/3: 339–60.

Vuong, Q. H. (1989) 'Likelihood Ratio Tests for Model Selection and Non-Nested Hypotheses', *Econometrica: Journal of the Econometric Society,* 57/2: 307–33.

Walgrave, L. and I. Aertsen (1996) 'Reintegrative Shaming and Restorative Justice', *European Journal on Criminal Policy and Research,* 4/4: 67–85.

Yazzie, R. and J. W. Zion (1996) 'Navajo Restorative Justice: The Law of Equality and Justice' in B. Galaway and J. Hudson (eds) *Restorative Justice: International Perspectives,* Montsey: Criminal Justice Press: 157–73.

Zehr, H. (1990) *Changing Lenses: A New Focus for Crime and Justice,* Scottdale: Herald Press.

Index